The Woman
Behind the Smile

Triumph Over the Ultimate Online Dating Betrayal

Debby Montgomery Johnson

Parker House Publishing
www.ParkerHouseBooks.com

Book design: Candi Parker
Editing: Judee Light
Cover photography: Cece Espeut
Published by ParkerHouseBooks.com

Urban Dictionary:

Catfished - Being deceived over Facebook as the deceiver professed their romantic feelings to his/her victim, but isn't who they say they are.

Having a fake Facebook profile, images and avatar in order to lure people to have romantic feelings. They are then catfished when the victim realizes the person they have fallen for via Facebook is not who they APPEAR to be.

Wikipedia:

Catfishing is a type of deceptive activity involving a person creating an online identity used for purposes of deception and social networking for nefarious purposes. The modern term originated from the 2010 American documentary *Catfish*.

When I was catfished back in 2010 there wasn't as much known about the underground world of online scammers and how they reeled in unsuspecting catches. I was newly widowed and very vulnerable. I believe that if I had been alerted to all of the "signs" that are online today, I would have acted differently, but I wasn't and I didn't.

I give you all of the signs in Chapter 10.

What people are saying...

We all have a part of us we hide from the world. This book is freedom in your hands - freedom to be authentic without fear of judgment, shame or guilt. Thank you, Debby, for showing us that we all are The Woman Behind the Smile.
~ Trish Carr, Author, Co-Founder of Women's Prosperity Network, Coach

When I first heard Debby's story I was completely in shock. I could not believe a woman of her stature and intellect could be duped in such a scandalous situation. This is a warning to all the people out there, men and women - Beware of the people that are hiding behind the Internet preying on those that are looking for love...
~ Wali Waiters, Executive Producer, Profiles Series Productions and "In View" Hosted by Larry King

This book is going to blow you away!!! Debby's story is so powerful and compelling that you will experience a wave of emotions from grief, to joy, to profound love and devastating heartbreak. Debby chose to become a victor and not a victim in an effort to serve others around the world. Amazing story!
~ Christy Rutherford, LIVE-UP Leadership

She had just buried her husband of 25 years, was trying to run his business without all the pieces of the puzzle, and felt responsible to be the rock for their four children. It is no wonder Debby Montgomery was vulnerable when she met what seemed to be a wonderful man online. For someone who was taking care of children and customers, here was someone who was going to take care of her, who might take some of the weight of the world off her shoulders. In reality, he was not who he appeared to be, who he very successfully pretended to be, and he took a lot more from Debby than the weight of the world. With courage and concern for others, she shares her story as a cautionary tale that should be read by anyone considering or in the midst of an online relationship.

~ Susan Law Corpany, Humorist, Speaker, and Author of
Shaking Down Santa

The headline read, "How I lost over a million dollars on a dating service"! I thought, I have to find out more. I reached out to Debby for an interview and she went on to tell her story. She told me that she had lost her husband and was picking up the pieces and that her friends and family were encouraging her to get back in the game so to speak. She found herself, of all places, on an online dating service. Was she vulnerable? Or was she just curious? Discovering someone she felt connected to, she was all in. All things checked out, after all she was an Air Force officer that was familiar with making sure all the dots lined up. And they did. He was very successful and talked a lot of his family and business dealings. Then he began to make requests. Still, she was confident in him and she started sending money because after all she was a caring and giving person. Then it begins to twist and she gets that feeling that something is terribly wrong. Then he said, "I need to tell you something."

After that she made a commitment to not let things get her down; she would become the woman with a smile. A MUST read for anyone on the dating scene, especially the online dating sites and for anyone that has faced adversity. This is a tale of courage and perseverance.

~ T. Allen Hanes, Best Selling Author and Radio Host

Dedication and Acknowledgements

I dedicate this book to those of us who put on a big smile and say, "Just FINE, thanks" when we answer the simple question – "How are you doing?" When in reality we are harboring a hurt deep inside that could be keeping us from being the wonderful people that we are meant to be. I started this journey because I wanted to alert women to the reality of online dating deception, but it has turned into so much more. I found my passion through some very traumatic events. I believe things happen for a reason and that we are eternal beings having a mortal experience. I hope you will find my experience as exasperating, exhilarating, and exciting as I did!

To my children, Christopher, Charlie, Jenny and Matthew, I want to thank you for letting me tell my story. I know it might be embarrassing or annoying to you, but when I realized that my story was a story that, if revealed, could help so many other people in the world, I had to tell it. I apologize for not listening to each of you throughout the "adventure" but maybe that was part of the process. I'm grateful that we have weathered the storm the last few years, and I'm grateful for your support going forward. I'm very proud of you all. I'm sorry dad died, but I know families are forever and we'll love you for eternity.

To my parents, Jack and Gwen, I couldn't have done this without you. You were with me from the very beginning of my life and have given me unconditional love and support ever since. I am truly sorry for pulling you into the most unbelievable experience of my life, and if there is anything in this account that hurts you in any way, please accept my apologies. I love you dearly and am so grateful you chose to be my eternal parents – with all of the earthly ups and downs.

To my brothers, sisters-in-law and a couple of close friends, I want to thank you for the many hours we talked about Eric. In spite of your apprehension, encouragement, cautions, and threatened calls to the authorities, you have always had my back. Thank you for loving me in spite of myself! You are my family and I love you.

To the strong women of the Women's Prosperity Network (WPN), Trish Carr, Susan Wiener and Nancy Matthews, and my friends in the Dedicated Entrepreneur group hosted by Sharon Lechter, who STRONGLY encouraged me to find my passion and to speak up, THANK YOU to all. Thank you for challenging me to look deep inside myself to first identify why I was wearing the mask, and second moving me forward with a purpose. There were times, and still are today, when I take two steps back, but you're always there to nudge me forward again.

To my sweet newlywed husband, Chris, thank you for loving me and all of the baggage that came along with me! Thank you for opening up to me on our very first date and allowing me to do the same with no judgment. When the girls at WPN encouraged me to speak out, you were the first in line to say YES...GO FOR IT! That support changed my life and I've been able to go forth in knowing that I am safe in your care. Hugs!

Contents

Chapter One

Behind the Mask

I've been thinking about Jane Jetson lately...she was the dutiful wife of George Jetson, from the 1960 television series, The Jetsons. She always tried to make life as pleasant as possible for her family. She was a stalwart member of society and even appreciated the Arts and the fine things of life. She kept up with her friends with their version of Skype, but on occasion she put on a mask. What was really behind that mask? Besides the curlers and makeup remover? Have you ever felt like you're living behind the mask of a "Strong Woman"?

I have and still do. I put on the smile each day and sometimes go about pretending my life is picture perfect. Why do I do that? Why do I think I need to do that? What is it that happened in my life that makes me think I can't show real emotions when things go "bad"? Why do I feel I need to be composed and in control all of the time? Was it the culture I grew up in? I'm certainly not going to blame the warm, loving and supportive family I grew up in or the quaint Vermont town I lived in. But could those have contributed to my living behind the mask?

Well, for the first time in my life, I feel like it's time to take off the mask and become the authentic woman that I really am. Yes, I'm strong...mentally, physically, emotionally, and spiritually, MOST of the time. But so often I put on the happy smile and the words "I'm fine" fly out of my mouth as if rehearsed on a daily basis. I'm fine because I want to be FINE...**F**ulfilled, **I**nspired, **N**aturally beautiful and **E**xceptional and I want to be fine because everyone else wants me to be **FINE!** But many times FINE means something less than fine! Fine means it's time to leave me alone with my problems and concerns. Fine means I'm okay but don't want to talk about it today. This is not a "tell all" book, but I feel it's important to tell some things because you cannot grow up holding "stuff" in for a lifetime.

I grew up in the small town of Woodstock, Vermont. There were only about 2,500 people in Woodstock, and we were the brunt of many jokes about how there were more cows in the town than people. I think people said that about the whole state of Vermont!! I loved living a mile out of town even though my parents didn't drive my brothers and me up and down Church Hill at every whim. We learned how to ride bikes at an early age or we walked through the woods to our friends' homes. In the 1960s we didn't worry about people hurting us like we worry about people harming our children today. We would leave home after breakfast and get to town or the country club and spend until dark with our friends. We didn't have cell phones and immediate access to mom and dad. If we needed something, we would go to dad's office at the Ottaquechee Health Center or we would find a pay phone and give mom a call. We were very self-sufficient children back then!

Although Woodstock was a resort town with many wealthy visitors throughout the year, the majority of us were year-round residents, and there was definitely an economic difference between the "locals" and the professional people who had come to town as doctors, lawyers and dentists.

My dad bought a dental practice back in the early 1960s after he served several years in Burlington, Vermont, as a dentist in the US Air Force. Although he, my mom, my older brother John and I moved to Woodstock and became an integral part of the town, we occasionally felt like outsiders. I think mom felt it the most, but she kept very busy at church and in civic organizations and was always taking meals to one old lady or another!

I learned how to serve others by watching my parents. I did the things I was supposed to do. I went to church on Sunday. I excelled in school academically and athletically. I played the flute in band and even held parts in drama presentations. I didn't feel like an outsider until I was around 14 when my older brother went away to private school and I was contemplating a move in that direction also. I remember my friends giving me a hard time about "being too good for them." I had always been on sports teams but was never part of the "popular" group. I was outgoing, friendly, kind, and the only thing I did differently than most of them was I'd go to Long Island every summer to stay with my grandparents and cousins. That was a treat and it got me out of town for at least a month. The only time my summer stay went sour was the year I wanted to get my ears pierced and my grandmother, a very opinionated Norwegian, wouldn't let me because "only the bad girls get holes in their ears" and that's not her language, that's mine!! Mom ended up coming down to get me early and we went and got our ears pierced together. I don't think Grandma ever thought of me in the same way again.

I went away to private school when I was 15 years old. I went to Phillips Exeter Academy, which was considered one of the top secondary schools in the country at the time. I didn't feel any more privileged or "better" than my friends at home. I just knew I could get a good education at Exeter and could play on the field hockey, squash, and tennis teams, and I was excited to go away. Except for two close girlfriends, I lost touch with most of my hometown friends.

The hardest part about leaving for Exeter came weeks before I was supposed to go. I was at church one night for a youth group meeting. It was January in Vermont and the temperatures were in the teens. It was freezing outside so my mom went out to warm up the car so she could come and get me. Mom went back in the house for a bit but soon noticed a very bright light coming from outside. Something exploded in our brand new station wagon that was parked in the garage, and it set the garage and part of the house on fire. As chance would have it, the all-volunteer fire department was off celebrating a wedding, and it would take some time for them to get notice and react. They did an extraordinary job of getting through the snow in our back yard to get water out of the swimming pool, but the garage was burned to the ground and the house was severely damaged by water and smoke. All of my things - clothes, stuffed animals, and books - which were laid out for school were ruined.

The smell of smoke was awful and to this day it makes me cringe. My family home was destroyed and it would never be the same. Thank goodness no one was hurt in the ordeal and I learned that family was more important than any THING in the world. My need for safety was sorely tested here and when I left for boarding school I felt very vulnerable and scared.

Part of my Exeter experience was realizing that I wasn't one of the smartest in the class and that everyone there had been like me - a big fish in a small pond, so to speak. Now we were minnows in a big pond and it was very intimidating. I couldn't get home often because we had Saturday classes and then games. I struggled with class work because for me it was like doing college work as a child. I didn't express my fears to my parents or to my friends at home because I didn't want to look like a whiner, and I certainly wasn't going to quit. I had to study harder than I ever had to before, and I was competitive to the bone and determined to be a success. I did so at the expense of spending my teenage years at home with my family. Looking back at this stage of my life, I am sorry for that because there are times when I believe my parents got to know my best friend at home better than they did me. That may not be true, but the thought makes me sad.

Throughout my adult life and multiple careers, I have been admonished to keep things quiet, confidential, SECRET (or TOP SECRET in my Air Force life). I always had to hold things in confidence so when it came to divulging what happened to me after dating online and other life events, I just did what I've always done...KEPT QUIET! I wanted to write my untold stories because my story is YOUR story. Each of us has a powerful event, at least one, from our past that we've kept hidden from others and have pushed to the back of our minds yet it's still in the front of our hearts and is in some way holding us back from being our true selves. I want to inspire you to uncover that story...remove your mask and STAND UP to your Power. Stand up for your heart, your health, and your happiness.

Before I can stand up to you, I need to sit down and reflect on how I've used the mask throughout my life to protect, to pretend, and to progress. I invite you to come along on my journey and make it your own journey.

How could a normally grounded, articulate, well-trained, intelligent woman be lured into a two-year online romance which would leave her emotionally and financially devastated? Why would she ignore admonitions from her family and closest friends and listen to the words of love and encouragement from a man she had never met and would never meet? What was it about the daily contact she had with her special man that trumped almost everything else in her life?

Wow, those are really good questions and the answer to them could be "I don't know!" But over time I've learned that I'm not the only one who has been emotionally manipulated because the heart ruled the head. However, I am going to be the one who will tell the story in hopes of keeping at least one more unsuspecting, trusting person from being ensnared by the international web of deception.

I may never know exactly WHY this happened to me, but I know there is a reason why I'm sharing this with you now. My story could be your story. My story has been real life for many others already, but it doesn't have to be anyone else's in the future. Pay attention to how subtle the web of deceit was woven in my story.

How in the world could you get so intertwined financially with someone you haven't met in person? How could he become such an integral part of your life? Those are a couple of questions many people have asked me over time, but let me tell you, things happened so gradually over

6

two years that for me the red flags were never there.

Everyone likes a "Once Upon a Time" story with the "And they lived happily ever after" ending. I do and I'm sure you do, too, so I'm going to give you one...at least one that starts with what you expect!

Once upon a time there lived a lovely woman who had just about everything that was important to her. She had the husband of over 25 years, four wonderful children, a loving extended family, good health and most of all, happiness and joy. Of course, there were some bumps in the road and not every day was spent eating bonbons and watching reality TV (ahhh, can you imagine that!), but for the most part, things were very good and that's what she wanted everyone around her to think.

Now, this story isn't going to reveal all of the hiccups encountered throughout my marriage. Anyone who has been married for more than one day will tell you that things happen and the romantic, hot relationship turns to comfortable, steady and sometimes just plain tolerable, but if you want it to survive and thrive, you do whatever you must to work on it. Married family life was one of the most important parts of my life because I had seen the joy and success of my parents' marriage for more than 50 years, and I so wanted to emulate that. Nothing was going to ruin what I valued as my greatest treasure...nothing until the day of "The Call"!

Chapter Two

The Call

"Mom, Where are you? Dad just died! I'm coming home to take care of everything."

OMG, I just came face to face with the most dramatic change in my life. The life that I had envisioned for myself and my family came to an abrupt end in a moment with one phone call.

How do you describe a day that starts off "normal" and turns into one of the worst days of your life? April 8, 2010, was that day for me and my family. It started off with "The Call"- actually many calls from my oldest son, Christopher, in Corpus Christi, Texas; my parents in Tarpon Springs, Florida; and the hospital in Hudson, Florida. Where Hudson, Florida was, I had no idea, but from this point on, I shall always have that town burned into my memories.

Right here and now, I could have easily climbed under a rock, hidden and admitted defeat, but instead, I was catapulted into the new stage of my life where I would stand up and make lemons out of lemonade, so to speak. I was, after all, the woman who always put on a smile and made sure life looked perfect. I had lived under the assumption that I was the strong woman that the world needed to see, and I had to keep on the mask in order to get through the next stage of my life.

But, I have to admit, once the shock of the call eased, I found myself having a flashback about all of the times I thought Lou should be eating better, exercising more, taking better care of himself and of me not nagging and instead holding things in because he had the choice to eat or do whatever he wanted with his weight. I hated contention and did just about everything to not engage in arguments, especially ones that didn't affect me – except that I did want my friend and husband of 25 years and the father of my four children to be alive for the next 30 years or more. In all honesty, it didn't surprise me that he had died, but it did surprise me that he went so suddenly and so young. Lou died on April 8, 2010 and he was almost 56 years old. He was 6'4" and weighed in at nearly 360 pounds. When we got married he was very handsome, fit, and 240 pounds. Over the years I hated that he gained so much weight, but I gave up trying to help him get to a more "normal" size. He was just a big man – in stature and in personality. He was bound and determined to do things his way, too!

I received "The Call" when I was attending the Annual End of Year meeting of Treasurers at the School District of Palm Beach County. I had taken a break around 10:00 a.m. and I looked at my phone. I usually don't check my phone during those meetings, but today I felt impressed to do so. Imagine my surprise when I saw a dozen missed calls and several texts and voice messages awaiting me.

Friends gathered around me when they saw the expression of grief that came to my face. My eyes welled up as I tried to find some place quiet to sit as I had to listen to Chris' phone call more than once to really understand the gravity of it.

"The Call" was to tell me that my husband had died...no notice, no uncontrolled illness...just in his words to an associate at the hotel where he was staying: "CALL 911, I'm having a heart attack!" And within 15 minutes he was pronounced dead in the ambulance.

I tried to stay composed, tried to stay in control, but I needed help. A couple of the girls collected my things and one drove my car home and two others drove me home. Once home, my head was swimming with all of the things I needed to do...

Call Chris and my parents back to let them know that I heard the news.

Pick up my youngest son, Matt, at high school BEFORE social media got the news.

Call the hospital and find out what I needed to do to identify his body...my parents ended up doing this as they lived only 30 minutes from where he died.

Figure out how to get Lou's body and belongings back from the Florida west coast because he had gone across the State the day before to get some work done on his treasured race car.

Call the funeral home to make arrangements...I never knew the cost of a memorial service could range from $1,000 to over $25,000.

Get the older kids to fly home immediately.

Breathe...sit down and breathe...this seemed to be the hardest thing to do.

Let others take over...that's what friends and family are for and for that I am eternally grateful.

The most important and most immediate thing I needed to do on that exhaustive list was to go pick up Matt at Park Vista High School. Although the kids aren't supposed to have cell phones at school, everyone knows they do, and everyone has Facebook or some other social media connected during the school day. I don't think I've ever gone with no notice to pick Matt up and that fact wasn't lost on him as he was called to the main office.

Our time in the school office was the first time I cried since finding out Lou died. When I saw my son, my guard immediately went down, and we held each other tight and sobbed. I cried for my sons. I cried for my daughter. I cried for myself because we didn't say goodbye. Lou had just left the day before to get his race car tuned up for the Homestead Miami race. We just gave each other a quick goodbye hug before he left. He wasn't supposed to NOT come back home. I cried mostly because my heart broke for my youngest son since he would be the one and only child living at home without his dad...he would be the one to feel the emptiness each and every day. Matt would never come home and see Dad sitting in his recliner watching Lonesome Dove EVER AGAIN. When we left the office we dried our tears quickly because it was time to put on the mask. I had to be strong for Matt and he felt now that he needed to be strong for me.

Reflections: Lesson learned here – let the tears flow and talk things out. I put up the mask here in order to hold things together, and I found out later on that the grieving period would find no closure if we didn't open up.

Chapter Three

The Funeral

Funeral preparations started the moment I arrived home from the Treasurer's meeting. There were already cars in the driveway, and I wondered out loud: "How did people hear about Lou dying?" Friends and neighbors were gathering around the kitchen counter and with everyone around I felt like I was in a bubble. All I could hear was "blah, blah, blah" noises coming from their mouths. I'd catch a question or two yet most of the noise was about what food was needed or what funeral home did I want to contact. I didn't have a clue at that point, but for most of our married life we had a binder called "Answers" which had lists of who to call if either one of us died, what songs were to be sung at a memorial service and by whom, and where we would be buried. What I didn't have were the particulars...but I had friends who knew just who to call, so I let them call.

Several of my closest friends had recently lost a parent or a sibling so they came prepared with the name and phone number of the funeral home they used. I gave up my control over to them and they made all of the calls. They knew enough about what had happened to ask the preliminary questions but then gave the phone to me to tell the particulars, such as what type of service would we have...would there be a burial or cremation...would there be any military honors and, if so, how many pall bearers would there be? What about getting Lou's body picked up from the west coast of Florida? What would that cost me? It's amazing how the costs varied between funeral homes and services. I knew Lou wouldn't want me to spend a fortune and I, frankly, didn't want to spend a lot because it dawned on me that he had canceled his $500K life insurance just two months ago because he thought the monthly premium of $500, which had just jumped from $100, was too much and he refused to pay that "just in case." I was very angry at him for being so shortsighted about the insurance, but I didn't want to fight with him. Again, I hated contention and to fight over life insurance premiums seemed stupid. He assured me that we had investments that would take care of us in our old age so there was no need to pay for a $500,000 plan "just in case he died." I knew I'd get a small VA stipend, and that turned out to be a whopping $250, which paid for the death certificates and not much else. Insurance, to have or have not, is a topic for another discussion.

As the afternoon went on, I was able to find the right funeral home for the right price. Then I had to pick a date for the funeral. Lou died on a Thursday morning, April 8, 2010, and I knew he wanted to be cremated so there would be no rush in having a memorial service, but I wanted to get it done as soon as possible. The kids would all fly in as soon as they could get flights, but my brothers and their families and many out of town friends would need time to get their schedules arranged to get to Florida.

I checked my calendar and saw that Charlie's Army flight school graduation was the next week. Lou and I had planned on driving up to Ft. Rucker, AL, to attend. I was dreading that drive because Lou was a very fast driver (he loved to go nearly 100 mph whenever he could), and I was usually scared and on the lookout for police officers. Lou was the only man I ever knew who knew how many points he had on his driving record at the Department of Motor Vehicles! He knew when he needed to slow down because another ticket or warning would suspend his license. In a way I was relieved that I didn't have to make the drive with him – what an awful thing to think because I loved traveling with the family. I loved FLYING with the family but in an airplane, not in Lou's Magnum.

I was so upset that I couldn't go to Charlie's graduation. Charlie getting his "Wings" was a milestone in his life and should have been one of the proudest in mine. I always felt he stood in the shadows of his older brother and for once in his life, he was being rewarded FIRST. Darn Dad...why did he have to ruin Charlie's special time and WHY did I have to miss it? I couldn't schedule the funeral for the middle of that next week so the three boys would take a road trip together to Ft. Rucker and that would be a bonding experience for them like no other. I'm grateful for that trip because they have not had a similar experience together since, but I am still mad I couldn't have gone, too.

I also couldn't plan the funeral for the middle of next week because it was Jenny's 19th birthday. What kind of a birthday present that would be for her...for the rest of her life? So instead I planned a small birthday party for her on Wednesday and made sure the out-of-town guests would come in afterwards. Again, I was the organizer and tried to make everyone else feel comfortable in spite of the agony I was going through myself. WHY did he have to die the week of her birthday? Why did I feel like this about my sweetie who just died? How could I be the birthday party planner and the funeral planner at the same time? As always, I put on the smile and became the "hostess with the mostest"!

The funeral took on a life of its own. Lou was a man of many lives, so to speak. He was a former USAF Missile Launch Officer and Intelligence Officer so he had friends from that time in his life that I needed to include in the planning. He had been the Bishop of our local church congregation, and we would need to use the building for the service so arrangements had to be made for that. He was also very involved in car racing and a member of several gun shooting clubs so members of those groups would need to be invited.

Then we had the family...my immediate and extended families would most certainly be present. There was no question that they would fly in for the weekend. However, Lou's family was another story. His parents had predeceased him, his older sister had severed relations in their early twenties, and the one occasion I had to meet her was "unpleasant" to put it mildly. There was NO way I'd ever tell her that Lou died. His younger sister and her husband, although we hadn't had much communication for several years, heard about his passing from Lou's stepmother and contacted me to get the particulars. They would come over from Ft. Myers, Florida, and wouldn't you know it, they arrived late. All invited...all due to arrive for the memorial service of the year because I would make it something people would remember for life.

Over 500 people attended the service. It was the most amazing celebration of life/memorial service and people came from all around the country. Friends from out west flew in just for the service and then caught a return flight home that afternoon. I didn't even get a minute to talk to them before they had to leave for the airport. The outpouring of love and affection was overwhelming for me.

The music played and sung by two longtime friends was beautiful and we made sure that Lou's favorite hymns, "Redeemer of Israel" and "High on a Mountain Top", were sung by the entire congregation.

Christopher, my oldest son; my dad, Jack; Kurt, one of Lou's best friends from his Air Force Intelligence team; several friends from church and I wanted to speak. Kurt talked about "the spy days" when he and Lou served as Intelligence Officers in Europe back in the 1980s, and the kids' eyes just opened wide as they hadn't heard about their dad's adventures. We weren't allowed to talk about our intelligence activities to the family, and even Lou and I were very selective in what we could tell each other about our jobs. I was an Air Force Intelligence Officer and I kept the secrets well throughout my career...the mask of secrecy prevailed and I was good at wearing it.

I'd like to include the text of my talk because it will give you more of an idea of who Lou was and how our lives intertwined over the years.

On behalf of my family I'd like to thank you all for coming today. I know Lou would want us to celebrate his moving on and I'm confident he is watching us with a great big smile on his face.

Lou and I met in December 1982 when we got to Intelligence training at Lowry Air Force Base in Denver, Colorado. He had just transferred into Air Force Intelligence after being a Missile Launch Officer in Great Falls, Montana, for 5 years. I was new to the Air Force and had just finished Officer Training School in Texas. I thought him to be funny, bold and somewhat of a pain as he was so self-assured and confident in all that he did. Our first real encounter was after I had given my first briefing to the class. I walked down the classroom aisle and asked him, "How did I do?" and he replied, "Nothing beats a great pair of legs!!" From then on I knew there was something special about him. Within a couple of weeks, as I was planning a class social at the Officers Club, I saw him sidled up to the bar. I went over to say hi and after a few minutes he said, "I don't say this to just anyone, but someday little girl, you're going to marry me!" I laughed and said, "Oh, Captain Montgomery, you're drunk." He said, "That may be true, but I don't say that to just anyone!" After dating for a few months and after we both got orders to Washington, DC, he proposed. We were married a year later in May 1984 in a beautiful ceremony in my hometown of Woodstock, Vermont. We joined the Church of Jesus Christ of Latter Day Saints almost a year later and were sealed together for time and all eternity in the Washington, DC, temple in March 1988. The last 27 years have been filled with joy, sorrow, laughter, adventure, and there hasn't been one year that we've been able to say on New Years that we were bored with our lives.

Lou made me laugh. He made me cry. I was in awe of his intelligence and wit but mostly by his kindness and generosity. He was opinionated and bold – you really loved him or you did not, but that was ok with him. He lived life to its fullest as he loved his family and friends. He loved his Magnum racing car and all of the guys associated with racing, but he loved our children with all of his heart, mind and soul and he would do anything for them. He had high expectations but only wanted them to choose the right, for he knew the consequences for choosing otherwise would not bring them joy. But he allowed them to choose for themselves as that is part of God's plan for each of us. His three phrases of wisdom to the kids were: 1: Father Knows Best (meaning Heavenly Father, not Lou!), 2: Truth or Consequences, and 3: Be the Best You Can Be. He tried to live up to those principles as he lived the gospel as best he could in his callings as Bishop, High Councilor, Stake Sunday School President, Home Teacher, and most importantly, father and husband.

What is he doing right now? I know with his insatiable curiosity for the answers to life's questions – the big ones like "Shall a man live again after he dies?" to "What is Truth?" to "Who shot JFK?", that he's in Heaven's mission training center sitting on the front row saying "BRING IT ON!" I know right now he is with his family on the other side of the veil. I know he is attending to his mother, father, our son John Henry, and playing with his very favorite kitty, Tiggy. I am grateful for our ancestors who rejoiced when he arrived on the other side as we have sought them out for many years. To his many friends, most of whom he considered brothers, I say, "Thank you." He loved you very much and I know he taught you many things including how to help me run his company.

I know that Families can be together again for Eternity. I know that he is preparing a place for me and the family to come and live with him again and that our separation will be for a brief moment in time. I know he loved me and I will always be grateful for the 27 years we had together and for our terrific children of whom he was immensely proud. Thank you all for coming today. God bless you.

The most reverent and honorable part of the service was when my sons, Christopher, a US Marine Corps Lieutenant, and Charlie, a US Army Warrant Officer, and my brother, Brad, a US Air Force Colonel, prepared the American flag for military honors. The silence in the room was overwhelming. You could hear a pin drop. I sat in the front row of the chapel – right in front of the casket – and watched in awe as they very carefully lifted, folded, tucked and saluted the flag. Every crease of the flag was made with precision and purpose. Charlie had served on a Funeral Honor Guard during his tour at Ft. Rucker and he knew the process by heart. But the emotions he and Chris held back were palpable. They were performing the last military honor they could for their dad here on earth and they were doing it with respect and love. I felt my heart burst with pride watching the boys and remembering the service rendered by their father for over 14 years. Charlie presented the folded flag to me and when the words, "On behalf of the President of the United States, the Department of the Air Force, and a grateful nation, we offer this flag for the faithful and dedicated service of Major Louis Albert Montgomery," were spoken, I just wept. For a moment I let my guard down and the mask of wife, mom, sister, and daughter went down and I was just a grieving widow. I looked up at the boys and the voice inside my head was screaming, "HOW COULD YOU DO THIS, POPPY?" but I kept silent and accepted the flag.

In silence the casket was moved out of the chapel into the hallway and outside to the awaiting hearse. The only reason we had a casket is because of the flag ceremony. You can't drape an American flag over a small urn. Lou had been cremated and his remains were in a metal urn inside of the casket. The urn was delivered to me sometime after the weekend. Although I tried to keep the costs of the funeral to a minimum, I did pay extra for the casket because the flag ceremony was a necessity in my eyes.

We moved on to an amazing reception where my friends had prepared food for all in attendance. I can't tell you what they had since I spent much of the next hour in the foyer greeting guests who had come from near and far – many of whom I didn't know but whose lives had been touched by Lou in some way. I know I didn't eat much throughout the day and adrenaline was keeping me upright and I have proof that I was there because pictures were taken and smiles were worn showing that I could now lead our family and we would move on. We believe that we are part of an eternal family and that families can be together forever, so on to the next chapter without Lou, at least in person.

Before I leave this chapter about the funeral week, I must speak about the food. Food was everywhere from the moment people found out that Lou died. Everyone showed up at the house with food of some sort in their hands. I guess, when we feel uncomfortable, we want to hold on to something comforting and for most people, that's food! I've never seen so much pasta in all of its forms...with sauce, with meatballs, with cheese, in salad, and in soup. I swear I'll never bring pasta to another home after a death. As the week went on, and I wasn't really eating anyway, my mom put pasta in freezer bags so that Matt and I would have something to eat in the next few weeks when everyone was gone. Believe me, I was very grateful for the gestures and the food brought fed the many people coming to visit, but...

Reflections: Hugs and chocolate might be a better gift next time! However, you only have to send a note or bring yourself unless asked to bring food. I was so grateful for all of the potluck dishes, rolls and desserts brought to the church after the funeral because my friends fed over 300 people and no one left hungry except for me. I ended up flitting around like a butterfly making sure everyone was taken care of. I wanted to make sure this celebration of life was truly memorable, in a good way, for everyone. Lou would have wanted it like that.

Chapter Four

Starting Over

The chaos and frenzy of the week's preparations came to a close as "regular life" started to take over. Within days of the funeral, the aunts and uncles, cousins, and friends returned to their homes and the two older boys returned to their military obligations. Jenny was the last to leave and I had a hard time letting her go. She willingly flew back to school in Idaho, but I knew she would rather stay home with me. I felt so bad that Lou had died right before her birthday. How could he have done that? He didn't ask me if he could die that week – Jenny was his baby girl and I know if he could have chosen a day to die it wouldn't have been the week of her 19th birthday. She will remember that week her whole life and probably not with fond memories. I contacted her friends and advisors to let them know she would be returning and anything they could do to comfort her would be appreciated. This is one time that I wish she had gone to school closer to home. So much with "Go away from Florida for school. There is so much more to life than the Sunshine State!" I knew she would be home for the summer in a month or so, so I felt confident all would be okay going back to her friends.

I put on the "I'm fine" mask as we drove 45 minutes to the airport in Ft. Lauderdale then I cried when I wrapped my arms around her at the airport - that's not unusual for me as I cry each and every time a family member leaves after a visit. The kids know that I'd tear up and they usually have a tissue ready for me -"Oh Mom, what a mush." I get choked up, can't talk for a moment, and shed a tear or two. I guess I get this from my mom because she does it too!

WHY DO WE PUT ON THE MASK of appearing in control when we really want to just let our emotions out to the people we love. Do we think it will make them uncomfortable? Do we think it will make THEM sad? Sometimes we just need a hug to get us through our saddest times, but we won't get that hug if we don't ask for it.

I always could count on hugs from the kids. Although Lou and I didn't hug as much anymore, with the kids gone and the house basically empty, I knew I wasn't going to get many more hugs and I was feeling starved for that close loving.

I went on autopilot for the next six months. I was thrust into the role of working single mom of four, with a company that belonged to my husband and no idea how to run it.

My parents stayed on for a while to support me emotionally and to help me focus on running Lou's company, Benfotiamine.Net, Inc. I realized that I had to run the company now because orders kept coming in and unless my dad told customers when they called that Lou had died, they obviously would have no idea that the President of the company had suddenly passed away. Customers were sad when they found out, but they still wanted their products shipped immediately and someone had to do that.

Lou had been asked one day by our largest wholesale customer "What happens if you die suddenly? Who would run your company then?" and I heard him say, "Oh, Debby will do that, and if she needs help, an associate of mine will be around to assist her." Lou told me at that point to make sure I took care of that wholesale customer first and foremost as the income from that account paid most of our bills! I asked him to write down instructions on what I should do and he did, but it consisted of a four-page document he called "Business Continuity Plan" and it only contained the basics, so I would have to call on customers, vendors, suppliers, and even Lou to help me figure out exactly how to run the company. I was bound and determined to honor his legacy and to make the most of a very viable business.

Inside, though, I was dying. I was mad that he didn't leave specific instructions on how to do the daily jobs. I had to go through emails to figure out how to order the raw products needed for production. We had no inventory tracker so I had to figure out how long my supply of finished product would last and when I needed to start another production run. I didn't want to deal with running out of product, because I knew people would be kind but wouldn't want to have their orders held up due to a shortage in the home office. I did run short once during that first year after Lou died, and I determined that I would NEVER do that again. My customers were appreciative that we didn't make them wait too long, but what stress it put on me because customer service is of upmost importance to me and I didn't want anyone mad at us!

I was frustrated that Lou didn't leave a list of passwords for his accounts. Thank goodness he was pretty consistent on which passwords he did use because I was able to figure out most of them when needed. But some days I sat at my desk and just looked at his picture and said, "Are you kidding? So, what is the darn password to this one?" He never responded directly, but I did get prompted to what might work.

My dad was a phenomenal assistant. Although he was 80 years old and a retired dentist, he took to the business and to helping me with purpose and ease. He answered sales calls and told the customers one by one what had happened to Lou…he established a rapport with the customers and made them feel like one of the family. To this day he does the same thing. That's a special quality he possesses, and outstanding customer service is what Benfotiamine.Net, Inc., is known for. Some days I feel bad for my mom because she became a "work widow" when dad was answering phone calls for me. Many days I hear her in the background because she sits in dad's office while he works. Maybe one day she'll take on the customer service position!!

For the next year I worked two jobs, 18 hours a day. I stayed on as Treasurer in the Palm Beach county school system for six hours/day mostly for the social interaction with my teacher friends but also for the medical benefits associated with that position. I worked directly for the Principal and took care of all school expenses and teacher requests. I was good at my job, but there wasn't enough work to keep me busy and I got very frustrated when I had to sit and wait for the six hours to end. I needed to be busy and sitting around just because drove me crazy, especially since I knew I was needed more at home with the company. I would walk the school hallways looking for teacher friends and always asked if I could help them. I even volunteered for lunch duty and that was a noisy job that nobody ever enjoyed!

When school was out for the summer, I earned more income in one month from Benfotiamine.Net, Inc., than I did from a whole year of working at the school, so I finally took a huge leap of faith and left the school district to run the company exclusively. I knew I would miss the social part of working at the school, because now I was a "solopreneur" and, except for the cats, there would be no one at home to chat with. I also had to pay for private medical insurance and the $6,000 deductible and the $700 a month premium had me stunned. My yearly visit to the doctor couldn't possibly be more than $200, but I couldn't take the chance of not having insurance and something catastrophic happen to either Matt or me, as that would wipe me out financially.

Reflections: Never look back and take that leap of faith! I put up the mask here because I thought I knew enough about running the company. I pretended to know everything, but I was really scared that I couldn't make things work. I relied on others around me and that was a very good thing, but it left me feeling more alone than before. If you are going to "fake it" just make sure you do it with a smile on your face. No one will know how unsure you really are!

I need to have control over things in my life – not in a freaky way, but in a practical, organized way. Why? I'm not exactly sure, but I like routine and routine means safety and order. Even when I was in the Air Force and was told by senior officers that I needed to change up my daily routines lest "the enemy" could track me, I basically stuck to my routines. When we lived in West Germany before the Berlin Wall went down in 1989, my friends and I, all Intelligence Officers with security clearances, felt a little paranoid sometimes when thinking we were being followed. I remember going into communist-controlled East Berlin to go shopping when the city was guarded by the Russians. We had to wear our Air Force uniforms while visiting, and we stuck out like a sore thumb. I knew we were being watched everywhere we went and that scared me. When I got back home, although I knew there weren't any Russians around, I drove the same way to work, to the gym and to shopping places in spite of being told to "change it up!" Oh, well! It's hard to change an "old dog"!

After Lou died, I found some control in my life on a daily basis when I went to the YMCA to swim laps. I'd go to work at the school from 6:30 a.m. until about 1:30 p.m. and I'd drive directly to the Y. At around 1:45 p.m., there wouldn't be too many people in the pool area. I guess here in South Florida the middle of the day was late lunch/early bird dinner or nap time for most of the elderly patrons of the Y, and the younger folks were still at work. This was a perfect time for me to do the ½ mile of laps that I felt I needed to stay in shape. Swimming was a regimen...a compulsive routine wherein I swam in the same lane, at the same time of day and tried to keep to myself except in my thoughts as I would "talk" to Lou as I went lap by lap. I, obviously, was talking to myself in my thoughts and to keep track of how many laps I was swimming, I made sure to do 10 laps of breast stroke, 10 laps of freestyle, 10 laps of back stroke and then some leg work laps. I'd do the exact same regimen day after day. Many days I'd cry while swimming in the pool because no one would know how heartbroken I really was and how terribly lonely I felt. I had my goggles so tight to keep the water out of my eyes that after swimming it would take an hour or two before the "scar" of the goggles went away and by then my red eyes would clear. I could put the "I'm fine" mask back on and go on my merry way without anyone knowing otherwise.

In spite of losing a lot of weight after Lou died, I still felt I was overweight, and there was no one around to make me eat, or make me do anything, as a matter of fact. There were days when I couldn't tell you if I ate breakfast or not. Some days I'd eat a handful of peanut M&Ms and figure that I had my protein so I was eating a balanced meal!

But my past started to haunt me. When I was a teenager and up through my college days, I was very heavy. My weight was always an issue and an emotional one at that. I hated going shopping for clothes with my mom because we had to shop in the women's section (for the larger size), and those clothes were so old fashioned. No matter what anyone said about polyester being easy to wash, elastic waists and stretchy pants were not what I wanted to wear.

I was told, "You're just big boned" or "Wow, you're such a strong young woman" or "You're so athletic", all of which I was, but I was really just heavy, and I hated that. I just wanted to be like my friends...skinny with long blond hair, clear skin and straight white teeth! Looking back I'm not sure any of my friends were skinny, blond or had clear skin or straight teeth, but that's what I thought the cool boys wanted so that's what I wanted!!

And now, 40 years later I looked in the mirror and I still felt heavy in spite of a very skinny body. One time a very close friend of Lou's came to visit and told me that I looked gaunt, and I was really offended. For the first time in my life I was down to 128 pounds, and at 5'8" I felt slim enough to wear skinny jeans. Lou's friend didn't see it that way and he let me know it.

I could never win at the weight game though because in my mind I was always too heavy, but in reality I got too skinny, and I'd get chastised for both. I did, however, finally see the need to take care of myself so that I could take care of my family. I had to stay in control, and swimming brought me the control I needed. I still have the same bones that I had back then, but I guess they're just not "as big" as before!

In addition to my daily routines, my nighttime routines were pretty regular, too. I'd work until the late hours of the night because I didn't like going to bed by myself. I'd crawl into bed around 1:00 a.m. and I'd only sleep on a quarter of our king-sized bed. I unfolded the covers only a quarter of the way, and Lou's side of the bed never changed except for when I changed the sheets on Saturdays. His side was always neatly made – military corners on the sheets included! In the middle of the night, my three cats found their way to Lou's side of the bed. At least there was something alive and warm lying beside me.

I found that nighttime brought the tears. It was the only time of the day that I couldn't stay distracted, and my thoughts turned to my life and how things weren't as they were supposed to be. I was sad because the future wouldn't be what we had planned. I was worried that I couldn't run the company like Lou would have. I struggled internally with the thought that after 25 years I wasn't married anymore, and I certainly didn't think of myself as single and I hated the word "widow" and all it meant. I hated when other widows would tell me I was part of the "Club"...a club of single women left behind by men who died. Wow, not my idea of a great club to belong to.

I also realized that I loved *the idea* of being married. And being married for 25 years was truly a success, but it wasn't always that great. For many years, Lou and I were roommates living in the same house for extended periods of time. We had developed different hobbies, different friends, and different interests, which I knew would leave us feeling apart when the kids all left the nest. I felt I had to put on the illusion that married life was "perfect" and that I was "FINE" at all times because that's what we girls do! Most couples do not want to admit they are not always happy with each other.

We weren't having marital issues serious enough to do anything about, but we could have done more to try to connect with each other. I missed the hugs and the little touches that made me feel close to him, and many times I felt like I was being left behind as he raced ahead of me and the kids when we went out. Perhaps he just walked fast because he had long legs, but I would have liked him to slow down and walk beside me instead of in front of me.

Look at Facebook and other social media and what do you see? Cranky couples celebrating their 25th wedding anniversaries in separate bedrooms or on separate vacations? Heck, NO!! Everyone is getting flowers or edible bouquets and chocolates! As a widow, I felt that people expected me to fall apart because, after all, my husband had died suddenly at age 55. I had no one to vent my frustrations to, to hug, or even look cross-eyed at, and so I had every excuse to fall apart. But, I NEEDED to be fine. I needed to put the mask up so that others would leave me alone. I needed them to leave me alone because I didn't want to appear weak or emotional. I'd be fine until someone asked me how I was doing, and then I'd start to tear up and for me that showed weakness. How could I tell others facing difficulties to "man up" if I, myself, fell apart at the simplest question: "How are you?"

I needed comfort, companionship, and love again because it had been years since Lou and I had really been "all love and roses!" I'm sure every married person can relate to this feeling. Marriage takes work and it's got to be more selfless than selfish. Unfortunately Lou had gotten involved with someone else for a brief time about 10 years before and, of course, no one knew about that because I needed to protect the family name and the kids. When he told me about it, many years later, I blamed myself for not taking care of him. I blamed myself because I spent so much time running the kids all around town for their sports and school events. I blamed myself for being too busy to be the best wife I could have been. After all, I did have four children within eight years (and two miscarriages in between.) I was a Cub Scout Den Mother. I had my mortgage license and attempted to help bring in some money to help out with bills. I took care of my mother-in-law for 9 years; I volunteered at the kids' schools and was VERY active in the ladies auxiliary at church. I thought I was the perfect wife and couldn't understand WHY anyone would want anything else. I tried my hardest to forgive and to not blame myself anymore; however, my trust in our marriage and in intimacy had taken a huge hit and when he started to put weight back on in a huge way, I felt like I wasn't that important to him anymore. I think he put the weight back on to protect himself from temptation again but he didn't realize that it made me feel like "chopped liver" and I HATE chopped liver.

Reflections: Being alone sucks, especially if you're still married, but worse if you're widowed. At least if your spouse is around, you have someone to look at – even if you're upset with him!

When friends said I needed to get back into life only six months after Lou's passing...to venture into dating again, all of my insecurities about dating when I was 16 came flooding back. I didn't like dating when I was young, and I knew I didn't want to do it now, but I wanted to show everyone that I could move on. In the deepest part of my heart and mind though, I still had a poor self-image. Remember I had been athletic but "solid" when I was a young woman, and when I looked in the mirror, I still saw that body – that 40 extra pounds hanging on my "big bones." When am I ever going to see my true self? In spite of being very thin now, I had to recreate myself to feel truly lovable physically. Can you see that this woman behind the smile has been in my life for a very long time?

I didn't fit into the married couples groups anymore...can you believe there were some wives, friends of mine, who got funny when I was around their husbands – even though we had been friends for 20 years and all I wanted to do was talk to a grown up human MAN once in a while! I certainly wasn't interested in someone they had complained about for 20 years!! I didn't consider myself single now since I had been married for so long and had my married name longer than my maiden name. I didn't drink alcohol or go to bars so the idea of that was out and the thought of dating again was not even a thought in my mind, although it was on my friends' minds constantly! What was I to do? I needed more to life than sitting behind a computer screen!

As a concession to my girlfriends, I looked into online dating. I felt it was a safer way to go rather than dating in person– at least for starters. At least with online dating I didn't have to worry about how my hair looked, or what I was wearing. I didn't have to compare myself to skinny blonds in the restaurant or be humiliated because my date looked at every 20-something that walked into the room. I looked at several dating sites for a week or so until I felt brave enough to set up an online profile. Of course I wanted to put my best foot forward and to create the best self that I could. I knew I was a "catch" but I came with lots of history, baggage as some might call it, including four children and three cats! At least three of the children were grown and living away from home so I hoped family was as important to the gentlemen as it was to me.

I couldn't believe how awful some of the eligible men were on the web. I found myself wondering if some of the guys who listed Master's Degrees on their profiles had actually finished elementary school – their writing skills were awful. Some of their profile pictures were very interesting, too...they showed up hugging other women and dressed in dirty clothes! What happened to civility, chivalry, and clean cut American men with good grammar? Wow, I guess I'd been isolated from the real world of men and dating for a long time, THANK GOODNESS, but my high expectations were not initially being met. I could have lowered those expectations, given up on dating, or just been patient and trolled along for a bit longer. My friends encouraged me to do the latter.

Reflections: Slow and steady wins the race! Don't lower your expectations, and remember the cream will rise to the top if you wait patiently!

"Try online dating!" was the call to action. So I did, and I took the path of least resistance and checked it out. I had seen the advertisements on TV and thought it would be a safe way to ease back into the "dating world." Well-meaning friends directed me to Match.Com, PlentyOfFish.com and some others, but I ended up setting up my profile on LDSPlanet.com, a Christian-based dating site. I knew other women who found their soul mates on this site and married them, so I thought it was safe and worth a try. I wanted to first find a special friend. I wanted to be loved again, but I was scared to put myself out there, subject to criticism or at least comparison. For over 25 years I had a big diamond on my finger and usually felt secure in my relationship. Now with knees shaking, I put up a very professional profile and made sure I looked "perfect". At least as perfect as a widowed mother of four with three cats and a dog could be. Wow, what baggage came along with my package, but I knew someone would love it!

Before I go on with my story, there are five facts about online dating that I'd like to visit. I found this research, written by Aaron Smith and Monica Anderson, on the Pew Research Center website, www.pewresearch.orgfact-tank, and find it quite interesting. I wish I had done more extensive research BEFORE I launched myself into the online dating world, but over the last five years so much more has been examined.

- Online dating has lost much of its stigma, and a majority of Americans now say online dating is a good way to meet people.

- Online dating has jumped among adults under age 25, as well as those in their late 50s and early 60s.

- One-third of people who have used online dating have NEVER actually gone on a date with someone they met on these sites.

- One in five daters have asked someone else to help them with their profile.

- 5% of Americans who are in a marriage or committed relationship say they met their significant other online.

Do any of these facts surprise you? I know I was very quiet about my online adventures. If someone asked me, "Are you dating yet?", I'd almost whisper, "Kind of...I have a profile on XYZ site" but I was a little shy unless I knew that the person asking was familiar with online dating. Then I could say, "Well, yes, and I'm having fun looking at all of the available men!"

When Aaron Smith and Monica Anderson first studied online dating habits in 2005, most Americans had little exposure to online dating or to the people who used it, and they tended to view it as a subpar way of meeting people. Today, nearly half of the public knows someone who uses online dating or who has met a spouse or partner via online dating – and attitudes toward online dating have grown progressively more positive.

Online dating fact #1: Online dating has lost much of its stigma, and a majority of Americans now say online dating is a good way to meet people.

I was once asked, "Tell us about how your family reacted when you first started dating online."

It's funny to think about the family reactions. My parents were the first to hear about it. Mom and I were in the Tampa airport when I first mentioned dating again and she got all giddy. She wanted me to be happy again and not alone. She knew I had loads of friends, but she knew the value of having a sweetheart to have and to hold. She and Dad had been married over 50 years at that point, and I wanted a relationship like they had.

However, I still thought my mother would be the most horrified, the one that would say, "This is ridiculous," but Mom had some girlfriends that were in their 70s and 80s who had actually done some online dating and found some wonderful men, so mom became my greatest supporter.

My brothers were told next, and they made me feel like I was standing in front of a firing line. I remember sitting in the living room of my younger brother's home, and the "boys" were on one side of the room and the "girls" were on the other. The seating arrangement turned out to be the support that I got! My brothers, two who were former Air Force Officers, and one, a large company president, sat me down and asked, "Who is this man? What do you know about him? We need to do a background check – we need to check out his financials." I looked over to the boys and thought, "Are you guys kidding? This is only dating!"

My sisters-in-law thought it was great! They thought it would be a fun adventure. I think they were going to live vicariously through me because they all had been married for over 15 years. They wanted me to be happy, but they knew it might not be easy starting over after so many years. I was grateful the girls were there to hold my hand going forward.

My children...they were hemming and hawing. The kids were very protective of me, and I'm not sure they were really ready for me to start seeing somebody other than their dad. They didn't want me to be alone, especially my youngest since he was going away to college, yet the possibility of my being with anyone but Dad was unsettling. I kept things quiet from the three oldest kids for a while since they weren't living at home anymore. The youngest, Matt, was still here, but he was very busy with football and school, and I'm sure he was happy that I was preoccupied with things other than him.

I went out to dinner with Matt each week and we used the "date" as training for when he was ready to officially date. I loved those date nights because we discussed so many topics, and it was the only time we got to sit and talk without others distracting us. I think the best dating advice I gave Matt was to leave his cell phone in the car or turned off in his pocket. There is nothing more disrespectful than your date pulling out a phone during dinner. What could possibly be more important than *you* at that moment (except for your mom calling!?) We usually practiced what I preached, but it can be challenging, even for the youngest of "US!"

Online dating fact #2: Online dating has jumped among adults under age 25, as well as those in their late 50s and early 60s.

The fact that online dating has jumped among adults under age 25 doesn't surprise me because they are the internet generation. They are mobile and have their phones attached at their hips! Online dating opportunities are easy and quick. You can be bold and sassy in the privacy of your home or on your phone.

Among my single women friends, aged 50 plus, almost ALL of them have ventured a little into the world of online dating. Some have had more success than others, but they all continue to at least look at the possibilities. I now act as their "gatekeeper" and make sure I play devil's advocate on this subject. I guess it takes one to know one, and on this subject, I'm the EXPERT!

Online dating fact #3: One-third of people who have used online dating have NEVER actually gone on a date with someone they met on these sites.

Why would you NOT meet in person when you finally decide to start dating again? This was a no-brainer for me, at least at first. It's scary to go on a date!! All of the insecurities that you've kept hidden inside start to surface when you're asked to meet someone for the first time. Now, at age 50-plus, I started to question the gray hairs that started popping up – even though I earned every one of those grays. I thought maybe I'd have to pull out the hair color before going out on a date UNLESS you don't meet in person! I never had to worry about my hair, or makeup, or what I was wearing. I hadn't learned to Skype and the guys can't see anything over the phone or through the computer...it's perfect when "hiding behind the mask" and we're always beautiful when we're in the eyes of the beholder or in the imagination of the magical, handsome, perfect-for-me man on the other end of cyberspace!

Reflections: Online dating may be viewed as a viable alternative to in-person dating, but unless you see the person in person...think twice, three times, a whole bunch before you commit to anything!

Online dating fact #4: One in five daters have asked someone else to help them with their profile.

You should NEVER do your own profile. I built a dating profile by myself and I went out there on faith. I wanted to be completely honest because that's what I thought online dating was about. I wanted to put my best foot forward, and

I expected the men to do the same. I put up some nice pictures – all with me in them but some with the family. I was completely transparent because I didn't want to scare anyone off. I came with four children, a business, a good education, and good career experiences, and I was a widow, my badge of courage.

My girlfriends came in and gave me a different perspective when they edited my profile. They added things that sounded better than I could have written. Why do we think less of ourselves than others do? Perhaps we don't think we are enough - pretty enough, smart enough, healthy enough, honest enough! Thank goodness for a little help from my friends and positive reinforcement!

Reflections: Do not post that you are a widow and own your own business. Somehow that information makes you a HUGE target for scammers...just wait and see how true this is!

Online dating fact #5: 5% of Americans who are in a marriage or committed relationship say they met their significant other online.

Several of my friends met and married the men they found online and they are very, very happy! But they rarely tell anyone the real story of how they met. We all want validation that we "did good" but going rogue with unconventional dating may not get you pats on the back. I wanted the same great outcome that my girlfriends had so I kept an open mind and an open heart. But I'd venture to guess though that this fact #5 is slightly low because I believe that there is still a stigma associated to the fact that you met your spouse or significant other through online dating!

Wow, I wish I had seen these facts before I got into online dating because they might have changed EVERYTHING that I did.

Reflections: If you found love and happiness through online dating or any other way of dating...own it and be proud that you found love. Each of us plays differently so enjoy the variety in life! But remember to keep your head in the game.

Chapter Five

The Connection Leads to Our Story

Back to my story. I posted my profile on a couple of online sites, but the one I thought would be best for me was a faith-based dating site. Several of my friends who were on that site met up with some very nice men, so if they could do it, so could I. Still scared silly, I sent out a couple of "invitations" to guys I thought were cute and good matches for me. However, it seemed that many of the men couldn't complete a full sentence in spite of having "advanced education/Masters" listed in the education part of their profile, and no one had taught them to use spell check! Nothing grates on me like spelling errors! I could excuse a few but, if there were more than two per sentence, I'd rather pass on that profile. (Please excuse any typos or errors in this book!)

You could set parameters for your search, and I was pretty particular. Lou was a good husband and I wanted to find someone who could match up mentally and spiritually to him. And it would be nice to find someone who was physically "put together" and could run and not be weary! I did NOT want to fight over weight this time around – neither his nor mine.

I started looking around at dating sites in September and on November 14, 2010, I received an interesting note from Talk2Me55@yahoo.com and it was linked to his profile. It was very intriguing.

The following list is in response to questions posed by the website:

Male	*Doctorate (education)*
55 years old	*Widowed*
5' 11" tall	
Average build	*Has 1 child, lives with 1*
Black hair - Black eyes	*Regularly attends church*
Caucasian	*Served a mission*
Very good looking	

A little about me...

I am in search of a long term relationship that after a great friendship is developed over time, hopefully it will lead to marriage, but only to the right lady. I'm not desperate or in a rush, but believe in leaving things to higher powers and know that when the time is right things will happen. I am fortunate that I am willing to relocate for the right person as well. Well there's not much to say as I would describe myself in one word as a man of good standards and policies that guides my entire life...I'm a very God fearing person who believes mostly in honesty, truth and faithfulness...I don't give up easily in everything I do and I've got a big heart for the best things in life. I'm a man of great taste who never settles for less. The keyword that guides my life is FAITH and there's nothing I do without its application...

How I feel about the Church...

I seek to get a lady who's truthful, honest, God fearing,

appreciative, understanding, humble, and extremely down-to-earth, a good listener and caring. I want one who's an epitome of beauty in heart. I'm not too concerned about the outward looks...All that interests me is the YOU-IN-YOU... I'm willing to give my entire heart to that special lady that fills these qualities...I don't expect a lady to be perfect but I expect her to be unique in her special way and I'm willing to accept her for who she is.

What I do for fun...

I love cooking and listening to music...All kinds of music except rock...I also love reading and watching movies too except I don't get to visit the cinemas always cos of the nature of my job...I love to unwind with my boy as he's my only surviving JEWEL...I also exercise for body fitness and that gives me time to engage in sports such as table tennis, running etc...I love dogs too.

(*disclaimer* This photo was sent to me by
Talk2Me55@yahoo.com.)

Well, this man seemed respectable, good looking and someone who might understand how life was after losing a spouse. I was quickly finding that people who were divorced looked at marriage differently than those of us who were widowed (still hate that word). I would fall hard and fast for the man that fit all of my prerequisites – and that included being tall enough for me to wear high heels again. Lou was 6' 3" and I, at 5' 8", could wear whatever shoes I wanted and he still towered over me! Why was that important? I wanted to look up to my guy, not straight ahead or down, that's all. He had to be at least as old as I, but I could bend on that by a couple of years. No cougar here! I didn't want someone with really young children because I had already raised four from birth, and I was getting ready to enjoy life as an empty nester.

I wanted someone kind, responsible, respectful of me as a woman and as a business person, and a real gentleman. Lou had a polarizing personality – most people either REALLY loved him or they didn't, and there weren't many in-betweens! I wanted my guy to be liked by my family and my friends. I didn't want to walk on egg shells when we went to visit family. I didn't want to make excuses for why my husband wasn't going to do something that he felt others were demanding of him – who knew doing the dishes was such an imposition.

This gentleman seemed to intrigue me with what he wrote, so I wrote a quick note back. A couple of days later I received this note and it was silly, but I felt very excited to have a "pen pal." My heart felt like it was bursting out of my chest...this reminded me of my crush days back in middle school!

Reflections: Writing is a great way to get to know someone; just make sure you do more than just writing!

Thanks for responding to my mails. You know my user name already from the dating site but just for the records, you can call me Eric Cole.

*   **This was the first thing I remember as being "odd"...why didn't he say "My name is Eric Cole"? But I chalked it up to his being British!***

I'd like to share a little about me as follows:

Well there's not much to say as I would describe myself in one word as a man of good standards and policies that guides my entire life...I'm a very God fearing person who believes mostly in honesty, truth and faithfulness. I don't give up easily in everything I do and I have got a big heart for the best things in life. I'm a man of great taste who never settles for less. The keyword that guides my life is FAITH and there's nothing I do without its application. The loss of my late wife (Sarah) was a painful experience especially knowing that I was about being a single parent with our son (Kenny). I never thought of seeking for love elsewhere because my mind was empty without her so I know what it feels like when making certain decisions out of proportion. My faith was tested during this period but am grateful to God for extending grace by using Mary who stood by me all the way being a mother figure to my jewel. I like to state here specifically for your knowledge that family is of great importance to me and I don't allow any obstacle to get in the way. Life is too short and all that matters to me is God being first and the people He has blessed me with. My world is revolved around my family and I love to extend this same grace to others by giving love at every given opportunity. There comes a time in a man's life when that emptiness is felt...Mine was deep and the only remedy is finding true love and companionship. Someone with whom you can laugh, cry, dance, walk, cook, sleep and wake, hug, care, help, pray, plan, succeed, excel, achieve, overcome, and build but most of all LOVE. We all need that special someone in our lives to make us complete.

The internet is a wide plain field which is the best and fastest means of networking all around the world so taking advantage of it is a bold step. I joined the dating site as a member and was introduced by my elder sister (Mary). I have heard and seen of couples finding true love and companionship through the dating site and so I thought it wise of seeking for that soul mate that will steal my heart away and guard it jealously. I am not a man who is desperate but believe in friendship built overtime on mutual trust and understanding and I do believe that equal minds think alike so my search is focused mainly on the inner beauty of that special lady. I care less about the physical attributes which could be regarded as a plus but seek more of the inner beauty that glows within. My life is incomplete without my faith and it has been a driving force that has helped me over the years so am believing that God will lead me to that special lady I truly deserve. Working as a general contractor for 30 yrs dealing majorly in supply of timber log products has been very profitable even though time consuming but I always get by because I have got passion for what I do provided it puts food on the table and pay the bills....LOL.

Please don't mind my being focused on me alone...I just enjoy expressing the in-depths of my heart so it can create an image in the reader's mind for better understanding in the spirit.

Just like everyone else we all have dreams. My dream is to reach out to the less privileged, poor, homeless, lost and needy all over the world winning them to Christ and impacting into their lives knowledge that will help them grow positively and making them responsible and useful to their world of contact thereby giving their lives a new meaning. Having all the wealth in this world cannot be measured by its numbers but true success is only measured by how many people one can affect positively and this is what we owe our world. I hope we can talk more extensively about this in our subsequent letters.

I hope this mail sheds more light about my personality. Please respond ASAP.

Remain blessed,
Eric

So why Eric Cole? He presented himself as a well-educated, well-traveled, hardworking business man from London. He had suffered the tragic death of his wife and he was taking care of his "jewel", his son Kenny, and his sister, Mary. I thought maybe their family might fit in nicely with mine.

Not bad for a first email, right? I felt he was being sincere...the language was a little "off" but I attributed that to his being from England! He had better grammar and spelling than many of the men who were online so I was happy.

I wrote back to Eric on November, 15, 2010...my mom's birthday! I wanted to be as informative as possible but also toss in a little "flirt" because that was the reason for connecting, wasn't it?

Reflections: Go easy on divulging too much information too soon in the game!

From then on Eric and I tried to write every day. We started writing notes on the dating site and then one day, early on, he said, "Look, I'm going overseas and I'm not going to be able to get on certain websites at specific times. Can we go on to Yahoo chat?"

Well, here I am again, technology challenged so I said, "Sure...just show me how to do it!" He got me onto Yahoo chat and from that point on we could talk all night long if we wanted to. Honestly, we chatted at the craziest hours because I'd be working all day at the school and home, and he was halfway around the world, so with the differences in time zones, night chats were "just what the doctor ordered!" There were many nights, around 2:00 a.m. or so, when I'd be just dozing off to sleep and I'd hear the ding, ding, ding of the Yahoo chat. My heart skipped a beat and I would literally run to the computer across the house to accept the call. We'd sit there and chat for an hour or two and that would get me through the alone times I felt while lying in bed.

Every now and again we'd talk on the phone and I heard his British accent – what a lovely accent it was, but he didn't stay on too long. I felt like I had my very own handsome, intelligent, and successful Brit, and that was delightful! I daydreamed of visiting his home in London and of going to see his extended family in Scotland. Wow, I allowed my mind to wander. Long distance would normally be a problem for a relationship, but it was actually safe for me. I had the excitement of falling in love again, but no pressure of developing a quick physical relationship. I felt like I was 15 again when I fell in love for the first time. I felt like my heart was going to burst through my chest, and butterflies raced through me when we chatted. I just needed to be appreciated and he made me smile – really SMILE!

However, it did get frustrating when we tried to plan a visit and for many reasons we couldn't make the plans work, but for now writing was okay.

I was a prolific writer and he would always write back – daily if possible, but always within two days. One of the most fun days we had was Thanksgiving Day, 2010, when my parents were here visiting for the holiday. "What a blast," I thought, "it would be describing the whole American Thanksgiving event to a man from London!" My dad was out and about cleaning up my garage for much of the day and my mom was in the kitchen chopping, sautéing, and preparing everything for our delicious and abundant family feast. I was on the computer for most of the day, in and out of the kitchen and it was so much fun sharing Thanksgiving. Try describing sweet potato casserole and stuffing a turkey to someone who doesn't cook and has not ever eaten such food! We spent almost eight hours on Yahoo chat, and that day we entered each other's lives in the most profound way and for the next two years we wrote our family histories together!

Eric and I spent nights together...hour upon hour writing through Yahoo messenger. We talked about everything that was happening in our lives. My daily life was rather routine with work, taking care of Matt and running Benfotiamine.Net, Inc., the best I knew how. His life was full of business ventures, trips to the ports in Malaysia, meetings with tax authorities, and anyone associated with moving his project forward. Our conversations were my only real social life.

I didn't fit into the "single" category and, like I've said, I hated the word "widow" and didn't want to be part of that group, although I was in spite of my wishes. I didn't fit into the "family" category at church anymore although technically I was married with children, but family to me meant mom, dad, and happy children.

Things were more comfortable with Eric and our online life. I talked to him about everything. He essentially became my confidant in all things. I suppose if I were to have seen a therapist to help me get over Lou's death I would have confided the same things I told Eric...I just saved myself thousands of dollars by talking to him!

Reflections: Journaling is a fantastic form of therapy and an incredible way to chronicle your life – a family history will be enjoyed by generations to come! I kept extensive journals because I felt I was writing my family history. I copied and pasted every instant message and email received from Eric for almost two years into my online journal, and I had these journals printed into hard copy books. I have over 4,100 printed pages. They are incredible!!

Early on in December, 2010, Eric sent me some poems that he said he sent from "my heart written and composed by me just for you"...I thought they were so sweet and that he was so talented!

"All My Heart"

You're the first thing I think of
Each morning when I rise.
You're the last thing I think of
Each night when I close my eyes.

You're in each thought I have
And every breath I take.
My feelings are growing stronger
With every move I make.

I want to prove I love you
But that's the hardest part.
So, I'm giving all I have to give
To you... I give my heart.
I am so glad I met you.

Debby Montgomery Johnson

"Lady of my Heart"

Spring comes with the sun
cold winds there are none
"Lady of my heart" - She's the one.

I gazed at her once
I gazed at her twice
this was the start of paradise.

She gazed back at me
She gazed lovingly
I heard the notes of a symphony.

We gazed at each other
and our daydreams took flight.

Spring comes with the sun
cold winds there are none
"Lady of my heart" - You're the one.

All I ever wanted is in you;
Love, laughter, a pillow for my fears.
I want to give and to be given to
So I might feel myself flow through the years
Alive in you, the wonder of my tears.

"An Autumn Story"

Autumn was it when we first met
Autumn is it what I can't forget

Autumn have made me alive
because in Autumn you entered my life

In Autumn you came like a summer breeze
I didn't realize what it is

In Autumn I fell in love at first sight
I knew that everything was alright

In Autumn there was that special dance
I knew our love will not have a chance

In Autumn I was under your spell
Autumn - a secret I will never tell

In Autumn you showed me pride
I wish I had never left your side

In Autumn miracles came true
everything I was longing for was you

That Autumn changed my life in many ways
I will never forget those special days

Autumn was it when we first met
Autumn is it what I can't forget

Reflections: Once your head rules your heart again, you'll find that the words written in the poems above are available through any Google search and they aren't written just for me by Eric. Hindsight is 20-20!

Throughout our correspondence Eric wrote the nicest things - things that felt right to my heart. I needed the loving sentiments that he expressed to get me through each day. I wanted to be worthy of his affections and, with each note, my heart was filled with joy.

Early on Eric and I were talking about one of his friends who was having trouble getting onto the online dating site where we met. Terry was his childhood friend, an architect working in Saudi Arabia, as well as other places around the world. I think the enrollment cost was around $45 and for some reason Terry couldn't get his payment to process. Eric asked if I would go ahead and send a check in to the site so that Terry could enjoy the companionship of someone like me! I was game and if Terry could have as much fun as Eric and I were having, what the heck...$45 wasn't too much for a friend. So I sent the check.

A month later all was great with Terry, or so Eric said, and Eric's next request was for me to set up a bank account for us so that he had an account where funds from his job overseas could be deposited before he arrived in person. The only way I could set up the account was to open it in my name with him as the beneficiary. Then when he got here we could make it a joint account for the two of us. I sent him the account number, the bank address and wire instructions so that he could instruct his company to wire money directly here. It was simple and easy, or so I thought. I had my "banking hat" on during this transaction and everything went smoothly, and I got to know so many of the bank personnel during this time.

Soon after I set up this account, Eric told me that he had spoken to his attorney, Peter, who suggested that in order to ensure a successful wire transfer between the bank in India and the account here that they needed to prepare a "Certificate of Ownership" which would be presented to the bank in India. This would, in general, let the Bank of India know it was okay to send the large sum of money to an account titled only in my name but on behalf of Eric Cole. The notarization and preparation would cost us 6,000 pounds. Hmmmm! Well, we then had our first little tiff and it was about finances. Now isn't that a surprise! I had to take a huge leap of faith and believe in Eric and his abilities and capabilities and trust that giving him some financial assistance would speed up his return home to me. I sent these funds via Western Union and had to split them into two different transactions. I went to Publix supermarket for the first transfer and the customer representative said, "That's a lot of money to be sending to Malaysia!" I told her that I had to get a friend home for the holidays and she believed me.

A few weeks after that, and right before Christmas, Eric asked me to help him with his flight back to the States. I knew he was short on funds because he was waiting for his job to finish up and then he would be paid a substantial payment. There was nothing unusual about this in my mind as I have had many orders where I put up the money first and then get paid at the end of production. It's the waiting to get paid at the end that's the hardest! This latest request was to be sent again via Western Union to a friend of Eric's in Malaysia. He and Eric were going to pick up the funds and then get to the airport to buy an airline ticket to Florida. As a banker I had never used Western Union for money transfers and I guess I was a little suspicious of using them, but they are very efficient and can deliver money pretty quickly around the world. I wanted to do this for Eric because I REALLY wanted him to come "home" and it was time to meet in person!

We got things ready for Eric to fly home and then I received a message that the shipping company was levying a tax on the shipment as it was sitting in port. Eric and Peter had to come up with a large sum of money to get the shipment released and once again they came to me. Eric told me that he hadn't had this tax levied against him before, but that it was a risk involved in their business and that's why the profits were so "mouthwatering"! He said that contractors were solely responsible for every expense incurred in the course of purchase and delivery and that he had to bear the brunt of the expenses until he delivered the shipment and all was accepted by the client. I did get to speak to him on the phone at this point because I needed to discuss this issue with him "in person". The telephone connection was awful but I heard his voice and it was British! All along I told him that I was a very prudent, cautious woman when it came to finances. He was very empathetic and convinced me that any financial support would be repaid as soon as he got home with me. My heart ruled my head on this front.

From this point on Eric, Peter, his attorney, and I encountered the most incredible obstacles while ensuring the tree delivery to the Indian clients. If there were tariffs or taxes to be levied, we paid them. If the port authorities needed extra paperwork, we had to get it to them. Nothing was easy, cheap, or done the way I expected it to be done here in the USA.

I had my share of corporate legal training when I worked as a paralegal in Denver in my early years and I had many years of banking experience when I was with World Savings and Wachovia banks just a few years ago but I had never encountered obstacles like these. I couldn't understand the WHYs to the delays or the huge amounts of money needed to reconcile the issues, but Eric continued to calm me down and encouraged me to help him so that he'd get home to me...that was my only goal at that point. He appreciated my support and gave me hugs from afar in spite of the knots twisting in my stomach.

My December 22, 2010, journal entry sums up how I felt right before Christmas. I felt this way many times throughout our journey together but I had invested my heart and soul and nothing was going to get me out of it.

"Well, as of yesterday I was ready to toss in the towel on my Brit...I was so frustrated with everything and so convinced that I'd never hear from him and then this morning there was an instant message from him waiting on my computer...saying he had internet connection troubles and he missed me and loved me. I'm an emotional roller coaster and this is very unsettling. I'm either a huge fool or this is going to be a wonderful relationship!"

On many occasions Eric listened so carefully to me and held me close to his heart in order to calm me. In the following communication, he was the shoulder I needed to lean on:

Eric: Are you scared? Tell me your fears baby.

Debby: I am a little scared that you may not be coming...and that's only because of the unknown...not having ever held you in my arms...and I don't want you to think I'm some unbalanced American woman (!) as I'm not...but this past week has had me off balance...I've never done the things that I did this week and my reasonable self is going NUTS as my heart is driving my actions and that's not usually me! So much of me is so in love with you and I can't imagine that you wouldn't be true to me. I really need a HUG! I'm sorry...I probably sound so neurotic...and I'm NOT!! lol

Eric: Sweetheart...Please listen to me. I just want you to know something here and now which I believe is very important in our relationship. I am your man and my love for you is endless. I wouldn't do anything to hurt you Debby. You are the one that befits my heart desire and if I say that I love and care about you then I will NEVER make you cry in pain but in love instead.

Who wouldn't melt with those words said to them? I was certainly disappointed with his not arriving for the holidays but for some reason my spirit was calmed just knowing he was there for me and he would be for almost two years.

Chapter Six

Getting to Know "The Family!"

All along I was interested in getting to know Eric's family because I believe that family is one of the most important parts of my life. Eric's parents were deceased and he only had one sister, Mary. I wanted to get to know Mary as soon as possible so that I could get an idea of what Eric was like – from her perspective! At first I asked if she had an email address. That would be the first and easiest way I could connect with her because she was living in England with Kenny, Eric's 10-year-old son. Eric always spoke fondly about Mary and Kenny.

After Sarah, Eric's wife, died, Mary was his "rock" and she took over the responsibilities of raising Kenny while Eric was traveling all over the world with business. Mary was also a widow and had never gotten over the death of her husband. She had five children and several grandchildren and she loved having them around, but she had a special bond with her "little brother"! I was excited to get to talk to her about Eric and to hear about his relationship with Sarah.

Eric and I started talking about family activities as the Christmas holidays approached that first year. Eric sent me pictures of his home in London and spoke of how Mary loved to decorate for the holidays. I especially love Christmas and go all out with lovely decorations. I put up a beautiful 10-foot Christmas tree every year, but I kept it up for over two Christmas seasons because I wanted Eric to see it!

Eric was so kind when he talked about Mary. He sent me a picture of her and said, "She is very homely and sweet." I believe he might have meant "homey" as Mary loved doing things around her home! He said she loved to "sing all around the house"! I thought that would be fun to have her sing as I play the piano, and we could make beautiful music together. Christmas together would be pure JOY!

(Photos provided by Eric Cole, Talk2Me55@yahoo.com)

Mary and I connected on multiple occasions and we became just like sisters. We talked about life after losing a spouse. We talked about raising our children. We talked about our spiritual experiences and how we wanted to go on in the future. Mary always questioned me about Eric and my intentions. I questioned her on his past and how he treated his wife Sarah. You can tell a lot about a man by the way he treats his mother and his sister. I asked her how he was as a father and if she thought he'd be good for me. We laughed out loud as we instant messaged each other for hours on end. She would be interrupted by Kenny and his antics and sometimes she would have him sit and write to me...that was fun as I got to know "my littlest son" and that's I began to think of him.

I couldn't afford all of the money transfers by myself, so Mary and I shared the agony of splitting the financial transactions that Eric had asked us to help him with. She was on a fixed income and had limited resources just as I did, but we always came up with the requested funds because we both believed in him. She sold jewelry just as I did. She lived modestly as did I. We were "kindred spirits" in many ways and we loved the same man...one as a brother and one as a future husband. I wanted to Skype with her and Kenny and asked to connect many times, but she said that she didn't have a good enough computer. She said that Eric promised her a new one when his job was completed. Wow, there were so many promises resting on the results of this overseas assignment.

Kenny and I had the most fun relationship because he interacted with me like any 10-year-old boy would. He'd come speeding into our conversations after Mary had him do his chores or before he had to get to his schoolwork. We'd be instant messaging at an incredibly fast pace...both of us type very quickly and we kept our conversations lively and full of teasing and fun. I enjoyed our discussions and I peppered him with LOTS of questions throughout as I needed to find out as much about the family as I could through him and Mary. I needed to validate the family as best I could so that I could keep things intact with Eric.

I sent Mary several packages and Kenny some postcards

from trips that I took with the kids at Poinciana Elementary. Interesting though, I got all of the letters and packages back from the UK with "addressee unknown" and each time I asked Eric what was going on he came up with a plausible excuse as to why the things were returned. The mail was just another frustrating but accepted part of our relationship.

Although I didn't go into dating with any thought of having more children to be responsible for, Kenny made me laugh and I felt like I'd be a good "mom" for him since Sarah had died when he was a little boy. My kids would be incredible big brothers and sister to him and even Matt mentioned on more than one occasion that he wished he had a younger sibling...one that he could have teased as the older kids did to him!

Although I have a terrific family of my own, I felt needed again...by a young boy that needed a mother, by a sister who needed a friend and by a sweet man who needed to be loved again. Family is a great thing!

Soon after Eric and I started writing, Matt and I went out to dinner and had a wonderful discussion about my dating again. I didn't beat around the bush this time and I asked him what he thought about my going out again. I told him that I was pretty picky and that I didn't want to start over financially. I wanted someone who "isn't broke"! I told him I needed someone well-educated and well-travelled. He seemed to understand and realized that Lou wouldn't want me to be by myself forever. We didn't talk specifics at first, but then I told him about Eric and his living in England. I asked Matt if he wanted to move to London. "Not really" was his response but he said he didn't mind if I were to do that after he left for college. I also asked if he would mind a younger brother. I know it sounds like things are moving too quickly, but I thought I'd throw it out so there wouldn't be any surprises in the event one day I brought someone home with kids younger than Matt. I never thought I'd entertain that idea, but I'm not too adverse to a child older than 10. I didn't want to scare Matt with this information, but I also didn't want to spring it on him one day out of the blue. He is a great young man. I asked him what Chris and Charlie might think. He had no idea about Chris, my consummate bachelor, but he thought Charlie may be more amenable as he was getting close to Amanda, his new girlfriend from Oklahoma! Jen would be fine at some point...just not tomorrow.

Chapter Seven

The Reveal – The Day My Life Changed

For almost two years Eric and I lived and loved our lives through email, instant messages, and occasional phone calls. We talked about everything, every day, for hours at a time. We planned on being together with our children for the rest of our lives.

At this point I'll revert to my actual journal. There is no way I could recreate the emotions of the "reveal" except to give you the actual words spoken between Eric and me on September 10, 2012. I will never forget that day. We first got into a very spiritual, spirited discussion. It lasted for hours before our internet got disconnected. Upon resuming our discussion this was said.

Eric: I remember the last question I asked you is what do you know about FORGIVENESS?

Debby: Yes and I answered that...did you get it?

Eric: Please send it to me again. Are you alone at home?

Debby: Yes.

Eric: Ok, good.

Debby: I am alone except for the SPIRIT, which is trying to keep me calm!

Eric: Yes, He is aware of this conversation as He led me in the first to initiate it

Debby: okay...

*Eric: I know this will break you down on the inside....You shared so much with me and I thank God you came my way but **I have a confession to make to you today, Debby,** and whatever decision you make, I will not blame you. But I want you to listen to my heart as this was done by the leading of the Holy Spirit residing in me.*

Debby: Okay, are you sure you want to continue?

*Eric: Yes please.....Now please know that this confession is not born out of my human flesh but by the Spirit. I am a born again Christian but I've wronged/offended you as my sister and friend before the Lord. This occurred to me when I was touched by the Spirit of God residing in me to stop and desist from my wrong deeds and live out my life in sincerity and truth as I was bought with a price by Christ Jesus and shouldn't be found living as Satan's seed...This revelation came to me not quite long ago and in humility, **I confess to you my wrong deeds of scamming you all along as it was selfish and inhuman especially to your kind and your love for Christ.** This isn't right and I was once blind but thanks be to God who has opened my eyes to see the light and retrace my steps from darkness unto His glorious LIGHT.*

Debby: THIS ISN'T TRUE...

Eric: Yes it is Debby....It is true.

Debby: I don't believe you...

Debby: Who are you then? Who is the dear man I've loved for the last 22 months?

Eric: It's sad but there is no Eric Cole.

Debby: There is...and I believe he is so distraught by our situation that he's making this up now...

Eric: This is the honest truth Debby. It's not a make-up.

   *Now the logical, intelligence officer, banker-trained Debby comes into the "real world"**

Debby: What have you done with all of the money that I've sent to you...to Eric? and to his family? What about Mary and Kenny? What about Peter and his family? I have too much information about your families to have this not be true. Why are you making this up now? After all these months?

Eric: There is no Peter, Mary or Kenny. It's all a make-up.

Debby: I DON'T BELIEVE IT.

Eric: It is true Debby.

Debby: Prove it to me.

Eric: My confession is the proof Debby. I wouldn't do this with my normal mind. Like I said, this was prompted by the leading of the Spirit of God. Let me show you who I am...let me come online in person to show you my real self...there is a camera on your computer and with yahoo chat I can come on live...let's connect.

Here is what I saw when we connected...

At this moment I was speechless. I can't believe I had the presence of mind to snap a picture with my phone.

Debby: How about your confessions about loving me all along? How about my giving you funds from my father? How about the notes written to my folks? This couldn't be all false. Why are you telling me this now?

Eric: Of a truth, I never intended to go this far or deep. But as time persisted, I developed passion for you and knew this wasn't right as you were a good lady and didn't deserve this kind of mal-treatment.

Eric: I am telling you this now because I was moved by the Spirit of God.

Debby: Then you need to make things right with me and with God.

Eric: That is exactly what I am doing Debby. But I have to begin by confessing to you and seeking for your **FORGIVENESS.**

Debby: What is your name? I still believe I'm talking to Eric.

Eric: JOSEPH.

Reflections: My emotions are just welling up inside me while I'm reading this confession in my journal. The last two years of my life were just ripped out from under me and this time I was responsible for part of it happening. What would I do now? I felt worse than when Lou died because I was a part of what happened. I look at his messages in the reveal and realize that his language is not the same as when he wrote to me before. I'm noticing the grammar, the word choices, the tone...this

isn't "my Eric" anymore. The way this man is writing I KNOW I would have thought him to be a scammer and a fake. I NEVER would have fallen for him and I never would have written to him for TWO YEARS and I NEVER would have sent him any money! NEVER!

Debby: I can forgive but it will be a hard thing for my family to do so if you don't make things right.

Eric: How can I make things right?

Debby: You need to return all of the money you took from me. I willingly gave it to Eric, Mary, Kenny and Peter but not to someone that wasn't honest with me.

Eric: Ok, but please I need to know if you've forgiven me.

Debby: Why is that so important to you?

Eric: It is right for me to do so by asking for forgiveness. It is our responsibility as Christians.

Debby: And it is right for Christians to make restitution after being forgiven?

Eric: Yes I totally agree with you on that.

Debby: Please tell me who you are...and where you are. If you return the funds so that I can move on with my family and my business then I'll be okay, whatever that means.

Eric: Debby I know this is so unbelievable right now but it is true and I am renewed especially now that I have confessed my sins.

Debby: I fell in love with Eric...and you must have some of his qualities...

Eric: It beats me on the inside to feel you suffer even now. I know that feeling of loss.

Debby: I have poured out my whole life to you...You know me better than anyone else... Eric, WHY ARE YOU DOING THIS TO ME?

Eric: I need to restitute with you Debby. I have wronged you and God is our witness. Please forgive me as I was a child but I've grown with a new mentality of Christ in me...The hope of GLORY!!

Debby: I will forgive you if you make good on everything I have done for you...I have family responsibilities, children that depend on me, parents that depend on me. I was DEPENDING on you for my future and now I need help. I was relying on the Spirit all along and I can't believe HE would lead me astray...

Eric: Yes I know and I am willing to do all you desire but I need to know if you have forgiven me. Please don't talk ill of the Spirit. There is a reason why God allowed this to happen.

Debby: Care to tell me why?

I have asked myself that question many, many times since Eric, or Joseph, tore the rug out from under me on that fateful day. It wasn't until I was interviewed in 2016 that a woman, a pastor from Indiana, said the following to me that I realized a possible WHY:

"I'm jumping. I'm shouting. I'm doing a lot of things. I'm a minister as well as an entrepreneur. This is what I want to say to you, Debby. This morning's inspirational message that God had me send out to my phone ministry said, 'Yea though I walk through the valley of the shadow of death, I fear no evil; for thou art with me...Thy rod and staff they comfort me.'

I know God had you in that valley. He knew. He set you there for a purpose for such a time as this. Though you say you didn't have the million dollars, you did have the million dollars. It was prepared for you to do what you needed to do to come forward so that you could share with us your story."

I was grateful for her feedback. I was grateful for her support of my cause. I was encouraged to continue speaking up because of her and the many other women that sent me emails and hugs from afar.

Why would God let this happen? As a very spiritual person I had to ask this question. I truly believe that things happen for a reason and in the eternal plan I had to live this story so that I could tell it to others. I hope it will help at least one person going forward!

Chapter Eight

Eric's Story

Somehow, since his confession, Eric is now "a new man" and full of the Spirit. This is his story of WHY he did this to me and once again, I believed it...do you? I can forever question the truthfulness of his story, but until I meet him in person I can only hope it was true. If not, then one day he'll have to account to a higher power.

Debby: I know that God is protecting me. I believed that Eric would, too, for the rest of my life.

Eric: I am sorry. I am repentant and this is why I am confessing to you.

Debby: Well, I thank you for that. Why did you do this? Really?

Eric: Thank you for asking. I will tell you everything so please, be patient with me as I open up to you.
I am a man who has had grievous experiences in my life and that majorly led me into doing what I did to you...There is certainly no excuse for stealing or deceiving others to become successful but by the time I finish with my story, I hope that the Spirit of God will communicate it deeper on the inside...I am the first born in my family of 6 and I lost my parents at a very young age...At the time, I was in the university and couldn't further my education because my parents weren't

able to sponsor for that. Initially, my family was doing well and we were so blessed with the gifts of life until the enemy came in and attacked us all. Poverty was the order of the day and that within a short while took away my father's life as he died of Hypertension. A few months after his death, my mother passed on. Please know that my mom was actually pregnant when we lost our dad and died after 2 weeks when she was put in bed...Like I told you, I am the first born and had six other siblings behind me...These ones were still little as at then and we were left and abandoned as orphans. Everyone we turned to left us to our fate and there was no hope...My parents never left us with inheritance or wealth that would have helped sustain us at least for a period of time so life was hell and very difficult for us all.

I lost everything and didn't know what to do and what step to take...My concern was majored only on my siblings because they were still little and I just needed someone out there to help cater for them on my behalf since every family member turned their backs against us...It was hard and the difficult times were distraught. As I speak with you, it's exactly 10 yrs since this happened...Luckily for me, some good Samaritan in my father's family who is my aunt came to their rescue...Though poor took them in and absorbed them even in her poverty and discomfort. Are you still with me?

Debby: Yes...I'm sorry about your family.

Eric: With that I was relieved and glad that they could at least have a home over their heads. Life went on for me as my predicament was personal and I was faced with so many challenges. As a young guy, I faced life in hardship and couldn't finish my education while in the university...I dropped out and needed to do something for a living...Found myself in bad company of friends and indulged in the advanced fee fraud or scam. Now I didn't do this because I enjoyed it. No one in his sane mind would take this as a job or profession...But the honest truth is that I needed to survive in the midst of the hardship and difficulties. I had siblings to take care of and no day passed by that I don't think of them and their well- being. Anyway, I gradually made some money from this so-called job and was able to send all of my siblings to a good school...a private one at that...I also rented an apartment and this was after few years where they all stayed as they were scattered around in different places.

I needed us to live together as ONE family and in unity so they can understand each other and learn to love each other instead of living apart and grow old...So I came up with the idea of getting an apartment which I did, thank God and ever since, we've all lived together as a family. As I speak with you, my immediate younger brother is almost done with his university education and I am very proud of that...My sisters are also almost done with secondary school education while the very last that was born few weeks before my mother's death is 10 yrs old this year and I've watched her grow from strength to strength.

Any money I made out of internet scams was channeled into investing in my siblings and giving them a good life...I also wanted to take up this sacrifice so that they all wouldn't find themselves doing the wrong stuff just to survive...I couldn't stand my sisters having to prostitute just to earn a living neither would I want my brother to be frustrated with life...So I took the blame. As I speak with you now, they are not aware of this confession that I'm making as I know it might lead to my arrest or whatever decision you might make but please know that even in fear and confusion, I am willing pay the price provided my siblings don't suffer. Love prompted me to do all that I did...This is essence behind the act...Not that I was proud of doing it or hurting other like you

But it was a means of survival...So I thought until you came my way and everything changed...Gradually my eyes saw the truth and when I realized that you were too good and a Christian. A child of God for that matter and I just knew something wasn't right...I felt the urge in me to stop whatever it was I was doing to you and this was what led to my confession today September 10th, 2012.

Debby: Have you done this to others too?

Eric: Yes I have, but not many.

Debby: Can you make good on what I sent you?

Eric: How do mean Debby?

Debby: Can you repay me what I sent over the last two years?

Eric: If my memories won't fail me, you have sent me well over a million dollars.

Debby: Yes, $1,080,762.43, plus interest.

Eric: Do I have that in hand right now as we speak? Honestly,

NO! Am I willing to pay it back? YES!! But I'd like to inform you on what I used the most part of the funds you sent me.

Debby: I hope you invested it wisely and made some money off of it because I have scrimped all along and have not really provided well for my own family. I did that out of love for a man I THOUGHT was going to be my future.

Eric: as you already know, I have responsibilities and they are my siblings. I helped feed and cater for them and their welfare. I also invested some of the money into businesses – some long term and some short.

Debby: That's nice...you realize that I sold my investments to help you.

Eric: Yes, I realize that Debby and like I said, I am willing to do whatever it takes but it had to begin with my confession and your forgiveness. I am at peace now with myself and I can move on.

Debby: I'm glad the confession has helped you come to peace with the situation. I'm a little unsettled about it though. My whole life for the last 2 years has been connected to you and the dream that I had a future with a man I respected and loved. I had dreams of a life with him and with his family. They were so dear to me. I have put my life on hold in so many ways waiting for Eric to get out of Asia.

HOW COULD YOU HAVE COME UP WITH THIS STORY? How could you have kept it going FOR SO LONG?

You have made me look like a fool to so many of my friends and family. The only way I can get through this is to have the funds back so I can carry on. If what you're telling me this time about your family is true then I won't report you, but you'll need to pay me back EVERY CENT and you'll need to assure me you will not do this to any other woman, EVER. This was just wrong...simply wrong.

Chapter Nine

The Money - Where Did You Get It?

You might be wondering where I got the money to help Eric. I am always stumped when I ask myself that question!

I ask myself over and over why I pulled together the funds every time Eric asked. I'm one of those "Damn Yankees" who was very frugal and tight with money in the past. I would willingly give to church and to the neighborhood kids' fundraising events, but I struggled with all of the panhandlers along the road and really got annoyed when my customers at the bank brought in "bogus" checks or scam letters. I rarely gave money to anyone other than close friends and family. So how could I do something to the magnitude that I did with Eric? Honestly, I got very creative.

When Lou died he had just canceled his life insurance – we had paid on several policies for more than 25 years but two months before he died he got mad that his premiums had shot up from $100 per month to over $500. He didn't believe in insurance to begin with, but we had four children and a mortgage, and I was only making $24,000 a year in my job and that wouldn't support us if anything happened to him. I tried to hide the fact that I kept the automatic payments going past the date he wanted to cancel, but he saw the deductions in my account and blew his top. I hated contention so I let him handle the fallout and that wasn't pretty for the persons on the other end of the phone at the insurance company. He insisted that we had enough savings and investments for any future needs, so I let him proceed as he wanted. Needless to say, when he died two months later I had no insurance to pay for expenses going forward. I could have been defeated and felt helpless, but, thank goodness, I had the company and I had put away some retirement money of my own.

Back to "HOW DID YOU PULL TOGETHER OVER A MILLION DOLLARS for your online relationship?"

I did everything I would have counseled anyone else NOT to do.

I cashed in my retirement accounts. I did so thinking I'd pay them back before the penalty would kick in. I looked at it as taking a loan against my own funds...little did I know I wasn't going to be able to pay them back, and I got hit with premature withdrawal penalties.

I went through all of my old jewelry and found things that I hadn't worn ever...selling gold for cash was the rage at this time and I knew there were pieces that none of the kids would want so I sold them for pennies on the dollar now that I look back at it.

I took loans against one of my diamond rings but this was a very temporary solution to getting funds quickly because I was bound and determined to NOT lose the ring to a jeweler. I did get to know the jewelers personally and promised them that one day when Eric got here that we'd return to purchase a big engagement ring when the time was right! That never materialized.

I got very creative with my corporate "receivables" and was able to move money around my accounts in order to complete Eric's requests and also to pay my bills. There were multiple times when I begged Eric to finish up his job so we could replenish my accounts. I felt he understood my anxiety and during those times he got Mary, his sister, more involved in offering up her funds. This brought Mary and I closer too as we messaged each other regularly on the progress of coming up with funds. I felt badly when she, also a widow, had to liquidate some of her stocks and sold family jewelry in order to help her "little brother." They had a very close relationship since both of their spouses had died and she supported Eric emotionally as well as financially. Or so I thought!

There are two things that I regret the most about my two-year relationship with Eric. The first was that I got my parents involved in one of the money requests. We were at the end of the adventure and Eric had his funds "on the way" to me, but there was a hold up and we had to come up with some temporary funding to get the money through customs. I asked my dad if he could help us, with the assurance that he would be paid back quickly. He said yes but wanted to make sure it was okay with mom. They had both been through a lot with me since Lou died, and they knew how much Eric meant to me so as any caring parents would do, they agreed to lend me the money with a good interest rate attached. It looked like a win-win for us all until the reveal came along and we all got sucked down.

The only positive about getting my folks involved is that we became VERY close because of the scam. I confided everything to them after Eric confessed, and they have been with me through every good and bad event since. I am so grateful for my mom and dad and I will be indebted to them forever.

The second thing that I most regret is that I didn't listen to my sons when they told me NOT to give Eric any money. They started on me in the very beginning of the relationship, and I believe the more they insisted I not help out, the more I helped. I told them that I was the adult in the family and that I could do what I wanted without their scolding. I stopped telling them anything about Eric from then on. Many years after Eric's confession and when I gained the courage to tell my story, I had to talk to the kids. I realized that the boys only wanted to protect me. They felt it was their duty to watch over me, and I took that away from them. I am truly sorry that I didn't listen – not because I lost the money, but because I lost their trust and it has taken much to gain it back.

Reflections: Con artists often insist that people wire money, especially overseas, because it's nearly impossible to reverse the transaction or trace the money. My sincere and firm advice - Don't wire money to strangers, to sellers who insist on wire transfers for payment, or to anyone who claims to be a relative or friend in an emergency and wants to keep the request a secret.

After a personal trauma, always have another person review your financials before embarking on any transfers. Have an objective partner, accountant, or friend be your advisor. I'm not sure this will prevent you from doing what I did. I was so self-sufficient that I kept others at arm's length when it came to finances, and even my accountant got caught up in the story of Eric's business and the promise of great returns once he got "home to the States." Listen to the still small voice of your conscience when parting with money. I could spend the next 200 pages of this book writing about the many money grams and wire transfers sent to Malaysia, London, India or wherever Eric and Peter needed them. I have documentation for every single one! In the end I had sent Eric and his family and associates over one million dollars. One million dollars...unbelievable! My records are thorough and extensive, and when I presented them to the FBI, their mouths literally dropped to the floor. However, even with all of the records, they couldn't help me – at all – because Eric (or Joseph) was in Nigeria and not in the United States. They did have me file a complaint with their Internet Crime Complaint Center (IC3), but that only put me in the system.

Chapter Ten

Scam Alert – Good-to-Know Information

Everyone says to be careful when you get involved in online dating. Over the years I've found little "tidbits" which might have signaled to me that Eric might not be exactly who he said he was. Even so, all along my heart ruled my head so I looked past these things. According to datingNmore.com, here are a few tips that "THEY MIGHT BE A SCAMMER IF..."

- Their last names are usually **Cole**, Moore, Smith or Williams.

- They say they are "God fearing" and search for "God fearing."

- They claim they are honest and caring.

- They immediately want to get off the website and onto Yahoo IM or MSN IM.

- Their grammar is not consistent with how Americans speak.

- They give you a phone number but it's typically a calling card or a call center; you can rarely get them on the phone.

- A majority of them claim to have lost a spouse/child/parent in a horrific traffic accident or airplane accident or if any of the above are sick or in the hospital.

Reflections: If you can't see the whites of their eyes, stay away! If I had seen this list before we started "dating", I might have been a little more cautious. No one told me to be wary of online predators...no one told me that widows were targeted by scammers. Why would I EVER suspect that someone would not tell the truth? My pictures were real. My information was honest. Look out – naïve, trusting Pollyanna here!

Chapter Eleven

The Interview- An Explanation

Tracy A. Hanes, of The Authority Syndicate, interviewed me recently and he had the following observations and questions:

Interview Question 1

"Deb, you literally have a picture. You made some decisions based on the picture. Can you describe that picture and what attracted you to it?"

Well, Eric had put this beautiful profile picture out online. He was 55 years old, appeared athletic and was nearly 6 feet tall. He had dark hair and dark brown eyes. He sent me a couple of photos and in all of them he was outdoors – in the mountains or just hanging out. I loved his smile. He looked so engaging and kind. He was a widower, a single father, and an independent businessman. He sent me pictures of his son, Kenny, and his sister, Mary. They also had a puppy and I got a picture of him! I received pictures of his house and he described each and every room. He gave me a "walking tour" around the rooms – especially his office and kitchen. He spent much of his time working and then spent a lot of time cooking with Kenny in the kitchen. Their favorite meal was pizza and Eric made a "delicious pie" according to Kenny. Their life just mirrored mine in so many ways and it was easy talking to my new friends. I could see myself fitting into their life and vice versa.

By profession, Eric was involved in brokering hardwood trees, meaning he set up deals between tree plantations and the consumer which was usually a large corporation. Right after we started chatting, he was awarded a huge contract with a company in Malaysia. He was to move thousands of exotic, hardwood trees from Malaysia to India. This job rang true to me because I have investments in hardwood trees in Costa Rica...go figure that! The job was to take him from Houston, where he was living at the time we connected online, to across "the pond" to the Far East. He was only supposed to be gone for a couple of weeks and because this was the holiday season, we expected him to finish up his business quickly and come back to the United States before Christmas. I was so excited as I had made plans to visit my parents over at Innisbrook Golf Resort in Tarpon Springs, Florida. Eric was going to join me there. I needed something "happy" to get me through the holidays because this was the first year without Lou. Eric would be a great distraction and a "heart help"!

Reflections: My December 1, 2010, journal entry provides some interesting insight into my state of mind at this time. Take note!

Matty and I just watched a wonderful movie...called "Keeping the Faith" with Ben Stiller and Ken Norton...it was fun, thought provoking, and heart touching. It made me realize that sometimes in life we have to take chances. In the movie, Ben Stiller (a Rabbi) had to defy "traditions" and take a chance on love with his long-time friend/girlfriend who was Catholic. It rocked his world, or so he thought, so he broke it off and they were both miserable...until he realized, through the help of his friend, who was a Catholic Priest and also in love with the same girl...that he needed to go for what was important and that was his love for his girl.

Happy endings are always wonderful! It made me realize that maybe I needed to take a chance, too. I wished Eric was around to talk to...it's scary thinking about moving on with another man...especially one who is from London and travels all over the world and one who has a 10-year-old son and a sister who is taking care of that son in London.

It's exciting and scary at the same time knowing that another man could really love me for me...a 52-year-old "hot mama" as Matty and his friends call me (ha-ha). I am putting this one in the Lord's hands...if it is meant to be, it will be and I need to trust that, so tonight I put my trust in God, in His plan for me, and say...let happen what will happen. I look forward to the future and all it might bring to me and the kids, and I know Lou is happy that I have gotten to this point in my life.

I love you, Lou, and I thank you for our life together and I thank you for putting me on the straight and narrow again. I know you want me to feel joy and love again. I know you know that I'm not replacing you and what we had...I'm just changing the plans a little and know that you'll be smiling down on me and will wait for me on the other side. I will love you always.

Interview Question 2

"This whole time, you are communicating with someone who you never saw live on Skype or in person. Is that correct?"

That's a true statement! The whole time Eric and I dated we never saw each other in person. The reason for this is because he was on a business trip overseas, and I thought that he was not in areas that had effective internet service. I must admit, I'm a little naïve as to how even the most third world countries have incredible access to the internet, Skype, Instant Messaging, etc. But because I have not been to Malaysia, or India, or some of the other places where he was working, I had to believe what he was telling me – that there was no internet service or sporadic, at best. I had no reason to NOT believe him, and I trusted that if he could come online and Skype that he would. We spent hours writing on IM and it was as if we were really talking. Most days I didn't even think about "seeing" him because I had his full attention. He and I typed very quickly and we kept up our conversations for hours and hours without breaks. He was a wonderful distraction from my worldly responsibilities. Our time together flew by and I had a smile on my face most of the time!

Interview Question 3

"You said that Eric was involved professionally in the hardwood business and that you own investment trees in Costa Rica. Do you think it was by design that he checked you out so well and that he was mirroring you?"

I don't think he could have known that much about me except for what I had on my profile. I absolutely know that there is so much information available to the public about each of us, but the fact that I had hardwood tree investments wasn't public knowledge. It's a little scary to me what people can find out about us with social media and background checks available for a small fee. However, Eric told me about his business before I ever divulged the fact that I owned hardwood trees. I checked out his company and their website. It was a fantastic website and all of the corporate contact information was there. So, I called the company! Here the intelligence training in me came out and I called to see if they had Eric Cole registered as a contractor in their system. I was surprised to hear the person on the telephone line say, "No, we don't have him listed" and then I thought that maybe independent contractors worked WITH the company instead of FOR the company and there might not be a listed affiliation. I rationalized at that point that there must be a reason for his not being recognized.

Interview Question 4

"Did you ever make arrangements to meet or rendezvous anywhere, or was your relationship just over the internet?"

Actually, we did make arrangements to meet. From the first month we were writing, we were making dates to get together. He would tell me that he was almost done with business and then we'd plan his travel to Florida. On several occasions I made hotel reservations at the local Hampton Inn. I even went over to the hotel a couple of times to check out suites because he was going to have Kenny and Mary fly here from London for the holidays so they could meet me and my family. I didn't have enough room at the house for all of them, and I knew they wanted some private time together. The Hampton Inn was accommodating and it was close enough to me but far enough for separate time. I made reservations multiple times but had to cancel them at the last moment as Eric's travel plans were canceled each time due to business delays.

Once there was a time when Eric was stuck in India, and he was arranging to have the money he was paid for his work shipped via courier to me. It sounded incredible but, instead of his getting paid via wire transfer, the Indian company was paying him in cash. While they were setting up the courier, he encountered a hiccup in the plans and the courier company needed my name on some paperwork. At that point I wanted so desperately to have him finish up that I was willing and able to fly to India to take care of things in person. I told Eric that I'd do that for us and in preparation for the trip I'd need a VISA to enter India. I flew to Houston, Texas, overnight and got a visa stamp in my passport! I had to walk the paperwork through the system and, thank goodness, everyone was very accommodating and efficient. I told them all about my story and they wanted to help me bring my guy home! I flew back to Florida the next day and then made arrangements to be met by members of my church in Mumbai, or Delhi, or wherever Eric wanted me to go. I knew I could trust them to keep me safe and to get me to Eric. I looked into getting a flight to India, and when I expressed my anxiety about the trip, Eric said, "Never mind. It's too dangerous over here and Peter and I don't want you in harm's way."

Again, I believed him, and I was so relieved that I didn't have to go. Even though many people travel to India and are completely safe, my oldest son went there on a student exchange and was almost mugged. I remember his saying that was one of the most frightening experiences in his life. I didn't want to experience that, so stateside I stayed! I did have that visa for six months in my passport before it expired, so I was ready!

I learned so much about international business from Eric. I didn't do much business on the Asian continent, so he told me everything he was doing and the frustrations he had with the local authorities. Some days I couldn't understand why he was having so many difficulties, but I used Google to verify what he was telling me – especially about FATF, the Financial Action Task Force, which is an intergovernmental body which develops and promotes policies to combat money laundering and terrorist financing. I got scared that he was dealing with that organization.

Interview Question 5

"At what point did all of this come to an 'oh, my gosh' moment and what did you do?"

I came to the "oh, my gosh" point almost two years into the relationship. It was September 10, 2012, and Eric came online that morning and said, "Deb, we've been chatting a lot today, and I need for you to tell me how you feel about forgiveness." I asked him "Why? Have I done anything wrong?" and he said "Well, I just need to hear what you have to say."

I put on my spiritual hat and we talked for hours about how I felt about forgiveness. Throughout our two years I had told him about things Lou had done and how I had to forgive him so that we could keep our family going strong. I had to forgive others that had made false statements about me when I was in the Air Force and I'm sure I had either said something or hurt someone without knowing throughout my lifetime so I had to learn how to ask for forgiveness. I went to my scriptures and to many of the books in my library which talked about others forgiving – even Christ as he said we must forgive others to be forgiven ourselves. Eric and I talked FOR HOURS about the subject and then our internet service got disconnected.

The time we were disconnected gave me a chance to regroup and really think about the subject of forgiveness. Had I really been able to forgive others in the past that had done things to me? Had I been able to ask for true forgiveness from those I might have offended? I remember Lou used to get upset with me when he thought I had done something, and I just said, "I'm sorry," and walked away. I know he didn't believe my apology was sincere, but I didn't want to prolong the contention, so a quick "I'm sorry" would usually suffice...or so I thought! I didn't understand WHY Eric had asked me about forgiveness at this point in our relationship. I thought I had done something to upset him. When he was able to reconnect, he had something to say to me!

Chapter Twelve

What Next?

Don Piper, author of *Heaven is Real* said the following:

"I may be knocked down, but I'm not going to be knocked out! Letting go of our old life is like jumping off a cliff into empty, dark nothingness. We're leaving behind the familiar and stepping into the unknown. It's a time of suffering and confusion. It's a process, and we have to go through the darkness before we emerge on the other side. The key is to use the time well, shifting our focus so instead of looking inward, bemoaning what we've lost and trying to figure out how we can deal with it, we begin to look outward, to someone who can heal us, guide us, and give us strength for our journey."

Since the collapse of my relationship with Eric, who I now know as Joseph, I spent several years hiding the fact that I even got involved in online dating. The only people who knew about the scam were my parents and several close friends. I hid everything from my children, my siblings and the world. I did go to the FBI's West Palm Beach, Florida, main office to report the scam and to give them all of the documents showing names, bank accounts for the money transfers, telephone numbers and my thousands of pages of emails and messages and, in spite of all of the information, they said they couldn't help me. I'm not sure if they really couldn't or just wouldn't, but in any event, they said unless Eric was in the United States, they couldn't do anything for me. The banks wouldn't even entertain my offer to give them account numbers and names because they said the transfers had been completed and they felt any accounts used for the scam had already been closed down. I decided that I had been so stupid, so naïve, so taken that I needed to put it behind me in a way that I could recover **in silence**.

But I couldn't, and I CAN'T. I was encouraged last year to speak up about my story. I needed to get it out to the women (and men) who needed it the most and those folks would be the millions that have been scammed themselves and are keeping it hidden...behind the mask of shame, betrayal, and fright.

Here an interesting fact – according to the FBI in West Palm Beach, Florida, there are more MEN scammed in million dollar internet dating schemes than women, so maybe I should be talking to the men!

With strong encouragement and support from my family and friends, I had to find my new normal. I had to believe that life had become different and that it could be better than before.

I am now coming out as "The Woman behind the Smile" with the mission of inspiring people to rise from relationship fraud, betrayal and mistrust. I want to show you how to remove the mask and uncover your truths and STAND UP in your Power! I have the vision to lead a worldwide women's movement to uncover our greatness from within, from which we'll move forward with love, gratitude and power to be the divine women we are meant to be.

For me, this new beginning is still challenging because even though I strive every day to be open with my feelings, I still fall back to hiding behind the mask. I know it's not good for me, so I make concerted efforts to open up. I can easily talk about the dating scam, but find it very hard to open up about living with a child afflicted by alcoholism and addiction due to his emotional hurts suffered because of his dad's passing. I believe that will be my next book. I take one step at a time in welcoming the freedom of letting go of the need to control something that I don't own.

The happy ending to my story is that I fell in love again. On October 30, 2015, I married a wonderful man who is supporting me in my mission. He understands that for me to be the best I can be, I need to STAND UP in the most positive, powerful, helpful way. Every day he reminds me to talk out my frustrations and to not hold things in. He is my safety net and my sounding board – when I choose to use it! He knows that my service to others will only make me a better wife, mother, daughter and friend. I am truly grateful for my second chance at love...this time with a real man, and I have seen the whites of his eyes!!

P.S. I have YET to get any of the money back from Joseph. I can only hope one day he will make restitution. Remember, he did tell me he would pay me back! By the way...if you happen to run across any of the people in the pictures included in this book, let them know they are being used by scammers, and I'm sorry for that.

****

If you or anyone you know is hiding something from the past or has been victim to internet dating fraud or to any fraudulent activity, I would love to hear your stories. If you know **anyone** who is involved in an online romance and you've heard them talk about their relationship and it sounds anything like my story, please have them contact me. I don't want anyone to go through what I did.

I want to take you from victim to victorious...from guilty to glorious...from angry to awesome! You will no longer be the Woman behind the Smile, but the Woman WITH the Smile! It could be your turn to take off the mask and become the woman you are meant to be.

Additionally, I welcome speaking engagements and can be reached at Debby@TheWomanBehindTheSmile.com.

> # Go now to
> # www.TheWomanBehindTheSmile.com
> ## and download the *free* brochure
> ## 7 Steps to Stand Up in Your Power

About the Author

Debby Montgomery Johnson is from Vermont and a graduate of Phillips Exeter Academy and the University of North Carolina-Chapel Hill. She is the President of Benfotiamine.Net, Inc., a vitamin supplement company that provides an alternative for the pain of neuropathy, a nerve disorder. (Benfotiamine.Net - Benfotiamine makes an extraordinary difference especially for diabetics and their families.)

Her background is diverse, from working as a paralegal and bank branch manager to being a U.S. Air Force officer, serving as an Intelligence Officer at the Pentagon, the Defense Intelligence Agency and in Wiesbaden, Germany.

Debby is just like you and she is a woman on a mission to live an authentic, joyful life as the Woman WITH the Smile rather than behind it.

Contact Debby at Debby@TheWomanBehindTheSmile.com or 561-512- 0824.